Her. Look in her face; look; is she like—?
      And forget in bliss thy sorrow

Admetus. O ye gods! What meaneth this?
      A marvel beyond dreams! The face—
         — 'tis she';
    mine, verily mine! Or doth God mock
            at me
      And blast my vision, with a mad
            surprise?

Heracles not so, this is thy wife before
          thine eyes.

Admetus Beware, the dead have phantoms
         that they send

Heracles nay, no ghost- raiser hast thou
        maid thy friend.

Admetus my wife, she whom I buried!

THE

TEMPLE SHAKESPEARE

By the kind permission of Messrs Macmillan & Co.
and W. Aldis Wright, Esq., the text here
used is that of the "Cambridge" Edition.

First issue of this Edition of "The Winter's Tale" printed 1894.   Reprinted 1895,
1897, 1898, 1900, 1901, 1902, 1903, 1904, 1905, 1905, 1906, 1908, 1909, 1910, 1912, 1914, 1919.

Shakespeare's Desk in the Birthplace.

SHAKESPEARE'S
COMEDY OF A
WINTER'S TALE

WITH PREFACE
GLOSSARY &c BY
ISRAEL GOLLANCZ
M·A

·LONDON : J·M·DENT · & · SONS · LD·
·NEW YORK · E·P·DUTTON & CO· MCMXIX

HP. βλέψον δ' ἐς αὐτήν, εἰ τί σοι δοκεῖ πρέπειν
     γυναικί· λύπης δ' εὐτυχῶν μεθίστασο.

ΑΔ. ὦ θεοί, τί λέξω ; θαῦμ' ἀνέλπιστον τόδε·
     γυναῖκα λεύσσω τήνδ' ἐμὴν ἐτητύμως,
     ἢ κέρτομός με θεοῦ τις ἐκπλήσσει χαρά ;

HP. οὐκ ἔστιν, ἀλλὰ τήνδ' ὁρᾷς δάμαρτα σήν.

ΑΔ. ὅρα γε μή τι φάσμα νερτέρων τόδ' ᾖ.

HP. οὐ ψυχαγωγὸν τόνδ' ἐποιήσω ξένον.

ΑΔ. ἀλλ' ἣν ἔθαπτον εἰσορῶ δάμαρτ' ἐμήν ;

HP. σάφ' ἴσθ'. ἀπιστεῖν δ' οὔ σε θαυμάζω τύχην.

ΑΔ. θίγω, προσείπω ζῶσαν ὡς δάμαρτ' ἐμήν ;

HP. πρόσειπ'. ἔχεις γὰρ πᾶν ὅσονπερ ἤθελες.

ΑΔ. ὦ φιλτάτης γυναικὸς ὄμμα καὶ δέμας,
     ἔχω σ' ἀέλπτως, οὔποτ' ὄψεσθαι δοκῶν.

EURIPIDES : ALCESTIS
(ll. 1121-1134).

Preface.

The First Edition. *The Winter's Tale* appeared for the first time in the First Folio, where it is the last of the 'Comedies.' It is perhaps the most carefully printed play in the Folio. At the end of the play the 'Names of the Actors' are given.

Date of Composition. (I.) Apart from considerations of style, the following facts make it almost certain that *The Winter's Tale* was one of Shakespeare's latest productions, and may safely be assigned to the years 1610-11 :—(i.) It is mentioned in the *Office-Book* of Sir Henry Herbert as an old play (" formerly allowed of Sir George Buck, and likewise by me on Mr. Hemming's word that there is nothing profane added or reformed, though the allowed book was missing, and therefore I returned it without a fee, this 19 of August 1623 "). Sir George Buck took possession of the office of Master of the Revels in August 1610. (ii.) Dr. Simon Forman in his '*Book of Plaies and Notes thereof* ' has a lengthy reference to a performance of this play at the Globe Theatre on May 15th, 1611. Judging by Forman's careful analysis of the plot, it must have been a new play at that time. (iii.) Ben Jonson mentions it with *The Tempest* in the Induction to his *Bartholomew Fair* (1612-1614): " If there be never a *Servant monster* i' the *Fayre*, who can help it, he sayes; nor of nest of *Antiques*? He is loth to make nature afraid in his *Plays*, like those that beget *Tales*, *Tempests*, and such like *Drolleries*."

(II.) Internal tests fully corroborate the external evidence:— (i.) With the exception of the prologue-like chorus scene of Act IV., no five-measure lines are rhymed; (ii.) run-on lines and double-endings abound; (iii.) the logical structure is 'more elliptical, involved, and perplexing than that of any other work of Shakespeare's'; (iv.) furthermore, the remarkable two-fold structure of the play gives to it the appearance of being one of Shakespeare's boldest experiments in dramatic art. "It is rare, if not unprecedented, in any art," observes Mr. Watkiss Lloyd, "to find an effective whole resulting from the blank opposition of two precisely counterbalanced halves when not united by common reference to some declared third magnitude. Nor is such a uniting power wanting in the present instance, whatever may appear to external view;" (v.) finally, there are the unmistakeable links connecting *The Winter's Tale* with *Pericles*, *Cymbeline*, and *The Tempest*, 'its companion and complement'—the Romances which belong to the close of the poet's life. On them all his gentle spirit seems to rest; 'Timon the misanthrope' no longer delights him; his visions are of human joy—scenes of forgiveness, reconciliation, and peace—a world where father is re-united with child, husband with wife, brother with brother, friend with friend. Like his own Miranda, Shakespeare in these Romances again finds the world beautiful:—

> 'O wonder!
> How many goodly creatures are there here!
> How beauteous mankind is! O brave new world
> That has such people in 't!'

The Sources of the Plot. The story of *The Winter's Tale* was derived from one of the most popular of Elizabethan novels, '*Pandosto: the Triumph of Time*' (or, *Dorastus and Fawnia*); "wherein," according to its modest title-page, " is discovered by a pleasant History, that although by the means of sinister fortune, Truth may be concealed, yet by Time in spite of fortune it is most manifestly revealed: pleasant for age to avoid drowsy thoughts, profitable for youth to eschew other wanton pastimes, and bringing to both a desired content. *Temporis filia veritas.*" * The book first appeared in 1588; its success may be gathered from the fact that no less than fourteen editions are known to have been issued. Its author was none other than the novelist Robert Greene, 'Maister of Artes in Cambridge,' whose death-bed utterances, reported in his ' *Groatsworth of Wit bought with a Million of Repentance,*' anticipated a veritable 'Triumph of Time,' save that *the absolute Johannes Factotum,* 'Maister of Artes in Neither University,' was destined to become, not in his own conceit, but by universal acclamation, 'the only Shake-scene in a country.' The 'scald, lying, trivial pamphlet' (as its apologetic publisher subsequently described it) could not have had reference to *The Winter's Tale,* at least in the form we know it; in all probability the old quarrel was altogether forgotten, Shakespeare certainly bore no resentment to Greene's memory, when he 'beautified himself' with the fine feathers of *Dorastus and Fawnia.*†

The Novel and the Play. Greene's then is the ground; Shakespeare's name is graven on the workmanship.

---

* Hazlitt's *Shakespeare's Library.* (*Cp.* Coleridge's adaptation.)

† A few critics are inclined to find a hit at Shakespeare in Marlowe's *Dido,* as finished by Nash, and adduce the following couplet as evidence that *The Winter's Tale* was an early play !! Æneas says:—

> ' *Who would not undergo all kinds of toil,*
> *To be well-stored with such a Winter's Tale?*

Some notable refinements due to the dramatist are the following :—(i.) in the novel Hermione's prototype actually dies upon hearing of the death of her son ; (ii.) her husband destroys himself, after becoming enamoured of his unknown daughter ; (iii.) the characters of Paulina, Autolycus, and Antigonus are entirely Shakespeare's ; (iv.) Hermione's character is ennobled throughout ; Shakespeare admits no 'incautiousness' on her part, no unqueenly condescension in meeting the charge ; (v.) Bohemia takes the place of Sicily, and *vice versa*, "apparently from a feeling that Bohemia carried better than Sicily, the associations of deserts and remoteness" ; finally, (vi.) the names are changed throughout :—Polixenes = Pandosto ; Leontes = Egistus ; Hermione = Bellaria ; Mamillius = Garinter ; Florizel = Dorastus ; Perdita = Fawnia. The Greek element in Shakespeare's list of names is striking, and should perhaps be considered in connexion with the Alcestis *motif* of the closing scene of the play. *The Winter's Tale*, from this latter point of view, suggests comparison with the 'tragi-comedy' of Euripides. One cannot but think that, by some means or other, directly or indirectly, Shakespeare owed his *dénouement* to the Greek dramatist,—certainly to the Greek story.*

---

* *Cp.* the passage quoted above, which has been translated as follows :—

> " *Hercules.*   Toward her turn thine eyes,
> And say if she resembleth not thy wife.
> Rest happy now, and all thy pains forget.
> *Admetus.* O ye immortal gods ! what can I say
> At this unhoped, unlooked for miracle ?
> Do I in truth behold my wife, or doth
> Some phantom of delight o'erpower my sense ?
> *Hercules.* This is no phantom but your own true wife.
> *Admetus.* Art sure she is no ghost from the nether world ?
> *Hercules.* You did not think a sorcerer was your guest. . .

Autolycus. Shakespeare's rogue has distinguished pedigree; his ancestor dwelt on Parnassus, where he was visited by his grandson Ulysses. A slight character sketch is given of him in Book XIX. of the *Odyssey*, 392-8 :—

> "*Autolycus, who th' art*
> *Of theft and swearing (not out of the heart*
> *But by equivocation) first adorn'd*
> *Your witty man withal, and was suborn'd*
> *By Jove's descend'nt, ingenious Mercury.*" *

Shakespeare, in all probability, first became acquainted with Autolycus in the pages of his favourite Ovid, perhaps in Golding's translation (*cp. Metamorphoses*, Bk. XI.).†

The Seaboard of Bohemia. Drummond of Hawthornden, in his famous '*Conversations*,' recorded that Ben Jonson said, "Shakespeare wanted art and sometimes sense, for in one of his plays he brought in a number of men saying they had suffered shipwreck in Bohemia, where is no sea nearly 100 miles." This censure has been frequently repeated. As a matter of fact, Shakespeare follows Greene in this geographical detail. He may

---

Admetus. O form and feature of my dearest wife,
　　　　　Against all hope thou once again art mine." (W. F. NEVINS.)

Observe, too, that Alcestis dare not speak to Admetus for three days; Hermione similarly "lives, though yet she speaks not"; when she does find voice, it is to call a blessing on Perdita; no word is addressed to Leontes. There are other remarkable parallels in the two plays.

* Chapman's paraphrase (pub. 1616); *cp.* "*My father named me Autolycus, who being as I am, littered under Mercury, was likewise a snapper up of unconsidered trifles.*"

† It is possible that Shakespeare's Autolycus owed something to Thomas Newbery's '*Book of Dives Pragmaticus*,' 1563 (reprinted in Huth's '*Fugitive Tracts*,' 1875).

or may not have known better; incongruities and anachronisms are not out of place in 'A Winter's Tale': he certainly bettered Greene's example, "making Whitsun pastorals, Christian burial, Guilio Romano, the Emperor of Russia, and Puritans singing psalms to hornpipes, all contemporary with the oracle of Delphi," —the *island* of Delphi!

Like the Chorus Time in the play, Romance might well claim:—

> "*It is in my power*
> *To o'erthrow law and in one self-born hour*
> *To plant and o'erwhelm custom.*" (Act IV. i. 7-9.)

The Duration of Action. *The Winter's Tale*, with its interval of sixteen years between two acts,* may be said, too, to mark the final overthrow of Time—the hallowed 'Unity of Time' —by its natural adversary, the Romantic Drama. The play recalls Sir Philip Sidney's criticism, in his *Apologie for Poetrie*, anent the crude romantic plays popular about 1580, when he outlined a plot somewhat analogous to that of *The Winter's Tale* as a typical instance of the abuse of dramatic decorum by lawless playwrights, who, contrary to academic rule, neglected both 'time and place.' *The Winter's Tale*, perhaps the very last of Shakespeare's comedies, appropriately emphasises, as it were, the essential elements of the triumph of the New over the Old. Sidney could not foresee, in 1580, the glorious future in store for the despised Cinderella of the playhouses,

> "NOW GROWN IN GRACE
> EQUAL WITH WONDERING."

* Eight days only are represented on the stage, with an interval of twenty-three days after Day 2 (Act II. sc. i.); and another short interval after Day 4 (Act. III. sc. ii.); the main interval of sixteen years comes between Acts III. and IV.; again, there is a short interval between Act IV. sc. iv. and Act V., *i.e.* the seventh and eighth days.

x

THE WINTER'S TALE

DRAMATIS PERSONÆ.

LEONTES, *king of Sicilia.*
MAMILLIUS, *young prince of Sicilia.*
CAMILLO,
ANTIGONUS, } *Four Lords of Sicilia.*
CLEOMENES,
DION,
POLIXENES, *king of Bohemia.*
FLORIZEL, *prince of Bohemia.*
ARCHIDAMUS, *a Lord of Bohemia.*
Old Shepherd, *reputed father of Perdita.*
Clown, *his son.*
AUTOLYCUS, *a rogue.*
A Mariner.
A Gaoler.

HERMIONE, *queen to Leontes.*
PERDITA, *daughter to Leontes and Hermione.*
PAULINA, *wife to Antigonus.*
EMILIA, *a lady attending on Hermione.*
MOPSA, } *Shepherdesses.*
DORCAS,

Other Lords and Gentlemen, Ladies, Officers, and
Servants, Shepherds, and Shepherdesses.

Time, as Chorus.

SCENE: *Partly in Sicilia, and partly in Bohemia.*

The Winter's Tale

Act First.

Scene I.

Antechamber in Leontes' palace.

Enter Camillo and Archidamus.

Arch. If you shall chance, Camillo, to visit
Bohemia, on the like occasion whereon my
services are now on foot, you shall see, as I
have said, great difference betwixt our Bohemia
and your Sicilia.

Cam. I think, this coming summer, the King of
Sicilia means to pay Bohemia the visitation
which he justly owes him.

Arch. Wherein our entertainment shall shame us we
will be justified in our loves; for indeed—   10

Cam. Beseech you,—

Arch. Verily, I speak it in the freedom of my

knowledge : we cannot with such magnificence
—in so rare—I know not what to say. We
will give you sleepy drinks, that your senses,
unintelligent of our insufficience, may, though
they cannot praise us, as little accuse us.

Cam. You pay a great deal too dear for what's given
freely.

Arch. Believe me, I speak as my understanding　20
instructs me, and as mine honesty puts it to
utterance.

Cam. Sicilia cannot show himself over-kind to
Bohemia. They were trained together in their
childhoods ; and there rooted betwixt them
then such an affection, which cannot choose
but branch now. Since their more mature
dignities and royal necessities made separation
of their society, their encounters, though not
personal, have been royally attorneyed with　30
interchange of gifts, letters, loving embassies ;
that they have seemed to be together, though
absent ; shook hands, as over a vast ; and em-
braced, as it were, from the ends of opposed
winds. The heavens continue their loves !

Arch. I think there is not in the world either malice
or matter to alter it. You have an unspeakable

comfort of your young prince Mamillius: it is
a gentleman of the greatest promise that ever
came into my note. 40

Cam. I very well agree with you in the hopes of
him: it is a gallant child; one that indeed
physics the subject, makes old hearts fresh:
they that went on crutches ere he was born
desire yet their life to see him a man.

Arch. Would they else be content to die?

Cam. Yes; if there were no other excuse why they
should desire to live.

Arch. If the king had no son, they would desire to
live on crutches till he had one. 50

         [Exeunt.

Scene II.

A room of state in the same.

Enter Leontes, Hermione, Mamillius, Polixenes, Camillo, and Attendants.

Pol. Nine changes of the watery star hath been
The shepherd's note since we have left our throne
Without a burthen: time as long again
Would be fill'd up, my brother, with our thanks;

And yet we should, for perpetuity,
Go hence in debt : and therefore, like a cipher,
Yet standing in rich place, I multiply
With one 'We thank you,' many thousands moe
That go before it.

Leon.　　　　　　　　Stay your thanks a while ;
And pay them when you part.

Pol.　　　　　　　　　　Sir, that 's to-morrow. 10
I am question'd by my fears, of what may chance
Or breed upon our absence ; that may blow
No sneaping winds at home, to make us say
'This is put forth too truly :' besides, I have stay'd
To tire your royalty.

Leon.　　　　　　　　We are tougher, brother,
Than you can put us to 't.

Pol.　　　　　　　　　　No longer stay.

Leon. One seven-night longer.

Pol.　　　　　　　　　Very sooth, to-morrow.

Leon. We 'll part the time between 's, then : and in
that I 'll no gainsaying.

Pol.　　　　　　　Press me not, beseech you, so.
There is no tongue that moves, none, none i' the
　　　world,　　　　　　　　　　　　　　20
So soon as yours could win me : so it should now,
Were there necessity in your request, although

4

'Twere needful I denied it. My affairs
Do even drag me homeward : which to hinder
Were in your love a whip to me ; my stay
To you a charge and trouble : to save both,
Farewell, our brother.

Leon.   Tongue-tied our queen ? speak you.

Her. I had thought, sir, to have held my peace until
You had drawn oaths from him not to stay. You, sir,
Charge him too coldly. Tell him, you are sure 30
All in Bohemia's well ; this satisfaction
The by-gone day proclaim'd : say this to him,
He's beat from his best ward.

Leon.   Well said, Hermione.

Her. To tell, he longs to see his son, were strong :
But let him say so then, and let him go ;
But let him swear so, and he shall not stay,
We'll thwack him hence with distaffs.
Yet of your royal presence I'll adventure
The borrow of a week. When at Bohemia
You take my lord, I'll give him my commission 40
To let him there a month behind the gest
Prefix'd for's parting : yet, good deed, Leontes,
I love thee not a jar o' the clock behind
What lady she her lord. You'll stay ?

Pol.   No, madam.

Her. Nay, but you will?

Pol.   I may not, verily.

Her. Verily!

    You put me off with limber vows; but I,

    Though you would seek to unsphere the stars with

        oaths,

    Should yet say 'Sir, no going.'   Verily,

    You shall not go: a lady's 'Verily' 's   50

    As potent as a lord's.   Will you go yet?

    Force me to keep you as a prisoner,

    Not like a guest; so you shall pay your fees

    When you depart, and save your thanks.   How

        say you?

    My prisoner? or my guest? by your dread 'Verily,'

    One of them you shall be.

Pol.   Your guest, then, madam:

    To be your prisoner should import offending;

    Which is for me less easy to commit

    Than you to punish.

Her.   Not your gaoler, then,

    But your kind hostess.   Come, I'll question you 60

    Of my lord's tricks and yours when you were boys:

    You were pretty lordings then?

Pol.   We were, fair queen,

Two lads that thought there was no more behind,
But such a day to-morrow as to-day,
And to be boy eternal.

Her.   Was not my lord
    The verier wag o' the two?

Pol. We were as twinn'd lambs that did frisk i' the sun,
And bleat the one at the other : what we changed
Was innocence for innocence ; we knew not
The doctrine of ill-doing, nor dream'd   70
That any did.   Had we pursued that life,
And our weak spirits ne'er been higher rear'd
With stronger blood, we should have answer'd heaven
Boldly 'not guilty ;' the imposition clear'd
Hereditary ours.

Her.   By this we gather
You have tripp'd since.

Pol.   O my most sacred lady !
Temptations have since then been born to's : for
In those unfledged days was my wife a girl ;
Your precious self had then not cross'd the eyes
Of my young play-fellow.

Her.   Grace to boot !   80
Of this make no conclusion, lest you say
Your queen and I are devils : yet go on ;
The offences we have made you do we 'll answer,

  If you first sinn'd with us, and that with us
  You did continue fault, and that you slipp'd not
  With any but with us.

Leon.   Is he won yet?

Her. He 'll stay, my lord.

Leon.   At my request he would not.
  Hermione, my dearest, thou never spokest
  To better purpose.

Her.   Never?

Leon.   Never, but once.

Her. What! have I twice said well? when was 't before?
  I prithee tell me; cram 's with praise, and make 's   91
  As fat as tame things: one good deed dying tongueless
  Slaughters a thousand waiting upon that.
  Our praises are our wages: you may ride 's
  With one soft kiss a thousand furlongs ere
  With spur we heat an acre. But to the goal:
  My last good deed was to entreat his stay:
  What was my first? it has an elder sister,
  Or I mistake you: O, would her name were Grace!
  But once before I spoke to the purpose: when?   100
  Nay, let me have 't; I long.

Leon.   Why, that was when
  Three crabbed months had sour'd themselves to death,
  Ere I could make thee open thy white hand,

And clap thyself my love : then didst thou utter
'I am yours for ever.'

Her.   'Tis Grace indeed.

Why, lo you now, I have spoke to the purpose twice :
The one for ever earn'd a royal husband ;
The other for some while a friend.

Leon.   [*Aside*]   Too hot, too hot !
To mingle friendship far is mingling bloods.
I have tremor cordis on me : my heart dances ;
But not for joy ; not joy.   This entertainment   111
May a free face put on, derive a liberty
From heartiness, from bounty, fertile bosom,
And well become the agent ; 't may, I grant ;
But to be paddling palms and pinching fingers,
As now they are, and making practised smiles,
As in a looking-glass, and then to sigh, as 'twere
The mort o' the deer ; O, that is entertainment
My bosom likes not, nor my brows !   Mamillius,
Art thou my boy ?

Mam.   Ay, my good lord.

Leon.   I' fecks !   120
Why, that's my bawcock. What, hast smutch'd
    thy nose ?
They say it is a copy out of mine.   Come, captain,
We must be neat ; not neat, but cleanly, captain :

And yet the steer, the heifer and the calf
Are all call'd neat.—Still virginalling
Upon his palm!—How now, you wanton calf!
Art thou my calf?

Mam.   Yes, if you will, my lord.

Leon. Thou want'st a rough pash and the shoots that I
        have,
To be full like me : yet they say we are
Almost as like as eggs ; women say so,   130
That will say any thing : but were they false
As o'er-dyed blacks, as wind, as waters, false
As dice are to be wish'd by one that fixes
No bourn 'twixt his and mine, yet were it true
To say this boy were like me.   Come, sir page,
Look on me with your welkin eye : sweet villain !
Most dear'st! my collop! Can thy dam?—may't be?—
Affection ! thy intention stabs the centre :
Thou dost make possible things not so held,
Communicatest with dreams ;—how can this be ?—
With what's unreal thou coactive art,   141
And fellow'st nothing : then 'tis very credent
Thou mayst co-join with something ; and thou dost,
And that beyond commission, and I find it,
And that to the infection of my brains
And hardening of my brows.

Pol.   What means Sicilia?
Her. He something seems unsettled.
Pol.   How, my lord!
    What cheer? how is 't with you, best brother?
Her.   You look
    As if you held a brow of much distraction:
    Are you moved, my lord?
Leon.   No, in good earnest. 150
    How sometimes nature will betray its folly,
    Its tenderness, and make itself a pastime
    To harder bosoms!   Looking on the lines
    Of my boy's face, methoughts I did recoil
    Twenty-three years, and saw myself unbreech'd,
    In my green velvet coat, my dagger muzzled
    Lest it should bite its master, and so prove,
    As ornaments oft do, too dangerous:
    How like, methought, I then was to this kernel,
    This squash, this gentleman.   Mine honest friend,
    Will you take eggs for money?   161
Mam. No, my lord, I 'll fight.
Leon. You will! why, happy man be 's dole! My brother,
    Are you so fond of your young prince, as we
    Do seem to be of ours?
Pol.   If at home, sir,
    He 's all my exercise, my mirth, my matter:

Now my sworn friend, and then mine enemy;
My parasite, my soldier, statesman, all:
He makes a July's day short as December;
And with his varying childness cures in me   170
Thoughts that would thick my blood.

Leon.   So stands this squire
Officed with me: we too will walk, my lord,
And leave you to your graver steps.   Hermione,
How thou lovest us, show in our brother's welcome:
Let what is dear in Sicily be cheap:
Next to thyself and my young rover, he 's
Apparent to my heart.

Her.   If you would seek us,
We are yours i' the garden: shall 's attend you there?

Leon. To your own bents dispose you: you 'll be found,
Be you beneath the sky. [*Aside*] I am angling now,
Though you perceive me not how I give line.   181
Go to, go to!
How she holds up the neb, the bill to him!
And arms her with the boldness of a wife
To her allowing husband!

       [*Exeunt Polixenes, Hermione, and Attendants.*
                 Gone already!
Inch-thick, knee-deep, o'er head and ears a fork'd
   one!

Go, play, boy, play : thy mother plays, and I
Play too ; but so disgraced a part, whose issue
Will hiss me to my grave : contempt and clamour
Will be my knell. Go, play, boy, play. There
    have been,   190
Or I am much deceived, cuckolds ere now ;
And many a man there is, even at this present,
Now, while I speak this, holds his wife by the arm,
That little thinks she has been sluiced in 's absence
And his pond fish'd by his next neighbour, by
Sir Smile, his neighbour : nay, there 's comfort in 't,
Whiles other men have gates and those gates open'd,
As mine, against their will.   Should all despair
That have revolted wives, the tenth of mankind
Would hang themselves.   Physic for 't there is none ;
It is a bawdy planet, that will strike   201
Where 'tis predominant ; and 'tis powerful, think it,
From east, west, north and south : be it concluded,
No barricado for a belly ; know 't ;
It will let in and out the enemy
With bag and baggage : many thousand on 's
Have the disease, and feel 't not. How now, boy !

Mam. I am like you, they say.

Leon.   Why, that 's some comfort.
    What, Camillo there ?

Cam. Ay, my good lord.

Leon. Go play, Mamillius; thou 'rt an honest man.

          [*Exit Mamillius.*

 Camillo, this great sir will yet stay longer.

Cam. You had much ado to make his anchor hold:

 When you cast out, it still came home.

Leon.   Didst note it?

Cam. He would not stay at your petitions; made

 His business more material

Leon.   Didst perceive it?

 [*Aside*] They 're here with me already; whispering,

   rounding

 ' Sicilia is a so-forth: ' 'tis far gone,

 When I shall gust it last.—How came 't, Camillo,

 That he did stay?

Cam.   At the good queen's entreaty. 220

Leon. At the queen's be 't: ' good ' should be pertinent;

 But, so it is, it is not. Was this taken

 By any understanding pate but thine?

 For thy conceit is soaking, will draw in

 More than the common blocks: not noted, is 't,

 But of the finer natures? by some severals

 Of head-piece extraordinary? lower messes

 Perchance are to this business purblind? say.

Cam. Business, my lord! I think most understand

Bohemia stays here longer.

Leon.   Ha!

Cam.   Stays here longer. 230

Leon. Ay, but why?

Cam. To satisfy your highness, and the entreaties
Of our most gracious mistress.

Leon.   Satisfy!
The entreaties of your mistress! satisfy!
Let that suffice. I have trusted thee, Camillo,
With all the nearest things to my heart, as well
My chamber-councils; wherein, priest-like, thou
Hast cleansed my bosom, I from thee departed
Thy penitent reform'd: but we have been
Deceived in thy integrity, deceived   240
In that which seems so.

Cam.   Be it forbid, my lord!

Leon. To bide upon 't, thou art not honest; or,
If thou inclinest that way, thou art a coward,
Which hoxes honesty behind, restraining
From course required; or else thou must be counted
A servant grafted in my serious trust
And therein negligent; or else a fool
That seest a game play'd home, the rich stake drawn,
And takest it all for jest.

Cam.   My gracious lord,

I may be negligent, foolish and fearful;   250
In every one of these no man is free,
But that his negligence, his folly, fear,
Among the infinite doings of the world,
Sometime puts forth.   In your affairs, my lord,
If ever I were wilful-negligent,
It was my folly; if industriously
I play'd the fool, it was my negligence,
Not weighing well the end; if ever fearful
To do a thing, where I the issue doubted,
Whereof the execution did cry out   260
Against the non-performance, 'twas a fear
Which oft infects the wisest : these, my lord,
Are such allow'd infirmities that honesty
Is never free of.   But, beseech your Grace,
Be plainer with me; let me know my trespass
By its own visage : if I then deny it,
'Tis none of mine.

Leon.   Ha' not you seen, Camillo,—
But that's past doubt, you have, or your eye-glass
Is thicker than a cuckold's horn,—or heard,—
For to a vision so apparent rumour   270
Cannot be mute,—or thought,—for cogitation
Resides not in that man that does not think,—
My wife is slippery?   If thou wilt confess,

    Or else be impudently negative,
    To have nor eyes nor ears nor thought, then say
    My wife's a hobby-horse; deserves a name
    As rank as any flax-wench that puts to
    Before her troth-plight: say't and justify't.

Cam. I would not be a stander-by to hear
    My sovereign mistress clouded so, without   280
    My present vengeance taken: 'shrew my heart,
    You never spoke what did become you less
    Than this; which to reiterate were sin
    As deep as that, though true.

Leon.   Is whispering nothing?
    Is leaning cheek to cheek? is meeting noses?
    Kissing with inside lip? stopping the career
    Of laughter with a sigh?—a note infallible
    Of breaking honesty;—horsing foot on foot?
    Skulking in corners? wishing clocks more swift?
    Hours, minutes? noon, midnight? and all eyes 290
    Blind with the pin and web but theirs, theirs only,
    That would unseen be wicked? is this nothing?
    Why, then the world and all that's in't is nothing;
    The covering sky is nothing; Bohemia nothing;
    My wife is nothing; nor nothing have these nothings,
    If this be nothing.

Cam.   Good my lord, be cured

Of this diseased opinion, and betimes;
For 'tis most dangerous.

Leon.   Say it be, 'tis true.

Cam. No, no, my lord.

Leon.   It is; you lie, you lie:
I say thou liest, Camillo, and I hate thee,   300
Pronounce thee a gross lout, a mindless slave,
Or else a hovering temporizer, that
Canst with thine eyes at once see good and evil,
Inclining to them both: were my wife's liver
Infected as her life, she would not live
The running of one glass.

Cam.   Who does infect her?

Leon. Why, he that wears her like her medal, hanging
About his neck, Bohemia: who, if I
Had servants true about me, that bare eyes
To see alike mine honour as their profits,   310
Their own particular thrifts, they would do that
Which should undo more doing: ay, and thou,
His cupbearer,—whom I from meaner form
Have bench'd and rear'd to worship, who mayst see
Plainly as heaven sees earth and earth sees heaven,
How I am gall'd,—mightst bespice a cup,
To give mine enemy a lasting wink;
Which draught to me were cordial.

Cam.   Sir, my lord,
　I could do this, and that with no rash potion,
　But with a lingering dram, that should not work 320
　Maliciously like poison : but I cannot
　Believe this crack to be in my dread mistress,
　So sovereignly being honourable.
　I have loved thee,——

Leon.   Make that thy question, and go rot !
　Dost think I am so muddy, so unsettled,
　To appoint myself in this vexation ; sully
　The purity and whiteness of my sheets,
　Which to preserve is sleep, which being spotted
　Is goads, thorns, nettles, tails of wasps ;
　Give scandal to the blood o' the prince my son, 330
　Who I do think is mine and love as mine,
　Without ripe moving to 't?   Would I do this ?
　Could man so blench ?

Cam.   I must believe you, sir :
　I do ; and will fetch off Bohemia for 't ;
　Provided that, when he 's removed, your highness
　Will take again your queen as yours at first,
　Even for your son's sake ; and thereby for sealing
　The injury of tongues in courts and kingdoms
　Known and allied to yours.

Leon.   Thou dost advise me

Even so as I mine own course have set down: 340
I 'll give no blemish to her honour, none.

Cam. My lord,
Go then; and with a countenance as clear
As friendship wears at feasts, keep with Bohemia
And with your queen.　I am his cupbearer:
If from me he have wholesome beverage,
Account me not your servant.

Leon.　　　　　　　　This is all:
Do 't, and thou hast the one half of my heart;
Do 't not, thou splitt'st thine own.

Cam.　　　　　　　I 'll do 't, my lord.

Leon. I will seem friendly, as thou hast advised me. 350
　　　　　　　　　　　　　　　　[*Exit.*

Cam. O miserable lady!　But, for me,
What case stand I in?　I must be the poisoner
Of good Polixenes: and my ground to do 't
Is the obedience to a master, one
Who, in rebellion with himself, will have
All that are his so too.　To do this deed,
Promotion follows.　If I could find example
Of thousands that had struck anointed kings
And flourish'd after, I 'ld not do 't; but since
Nor brass nor stone nor parchment bears not one, 360
Let villany itself forswear 't.　I must

Forsake the court : to do 't, or no, is certain
To me a break-neck.   Happy star reign now !
Here comes Bohemia.

Re-enter Polixenes.

Pol.   This is strange : methinks
My favour here begins to warp.   Not speak ?
Good day, Camillo.

Cam.   Hail, most royal sir !

Pol. What is the news i' the court ?

Cam.   None rare, my lord.

Pol. The king hath on him such a countenance
As he had lost some province, and a region
Loved as he loves himself : even now I met him 370
With customary compliment ; when he,
Wafting his eyes to the contrary, and falling
A lip of much contempt, speeds from me and
So leaves me, to consider what is breeding
That changes thus his manners.

Cam. I dare not know, my lord.

Pol. How ! dare not ! do not. Do you know, and dare
    not ?
Be intelligent to me : 'tis thereabouts ;
For, to yourself, what you do know, you must,
And cannot say, you dare not. Good Camillo, 380

Your changed complexions are to me a mirror
Which shows me mine changed too; for I must be
A party in this alteration, finding
Myself thus alter'd with 't.

Cam.   There is a sickness
Which puts some of us in distemper; but
I cannot name the disease; and it is caught
Of you that yet are well.

Pol.   How! caught of me!
Make me not sighted like the basilisk:
I have look'd on thousands, who have sped the better
By my regard, but kill'd none so.   Camillo,— 390
As you are certainly a gentleman; thereto
Clerk-like experienced, which no less adorns
Our gentry than our parents' noble names,
In whose success we are gentle,—I beseech you,
If you know aught which does behove my knowledge
Thereof to be inform'd, imprison 't not
In ignorant concealment.

Cam.   I may not answer.

Pol. A sickness caught of me, and yet I well!
I must be answer'd.   Dost thou hear, Camillo?
I conjure thee, by all the parts of man   400
Which honour does acknowledge, whereof the least
Is not this suit of mine, that thou declare

What incidency thou dost guess of harm
Is creeping toward me; how far off, how near:
Which way to be prevented, if to be;
If not, how best to bear it.

Cam.   Sir, I will tell you;
Since I am charged in honour and by him
That I think honourable: therefore mark my counsel,
Which must be ev'n as swiftly follow'd as
I mean to utter it, or both yourself and me   410
Cry lost, and so good night!

Pol.   On, good Camillo.

Cam. I am appointed him to murder you.

Pol. By whom, Camillo?

Cam.   By the king.

Pol.   For what?

Cam. He thinks, nay, with all confidence he swears,
As he had seen 't, or been an instrument
To vice you to 't, that you have touch'd his queen
Forbiddenly.

Pol.   O then, my best blood turn
To an infected jelly, and my name
Be yoked with his that did betray the Best!
Turn then my freshest reputation to   420
A savour that may strike the dullest nostril
Where I arrive, and my approach be shunn'd,

23

Nay, hated too, worse than the great'st infection
That e'er was heard or read!

Cam.   Swear his thought over
By each particular star in heaven and
By all their influences, you may as well
Forbid the sea for to obey the moon,
As or by oath remove or counsel shake
The fabric of his folly, whose foundation
Is piled upon his faith, and will continue   430
The standing of his body.

Pol.   How should this grow?

Cam. I know not: but I am sure 'tis safer to
Avoid what's grown than question how 'tis born.
If therefore you dare trust my honesty,
That lies enclosed in this trunk which you
Shall bear along impawn'd, away to-night!
Your followers I will whisper to the business;
And will by twos and threes at several posterns,
Clear them o' the city.   For myself, I 'll put
My fortunes to your service, which are here   440
By this discovery lost.   Be not uncertain;
For, by the honour of my parents, I
Have utter'd truth: which if you seek to prove,
I dare not stand by; nor shall you be safer
That one condemn'd by the king's own mouth, thereon

His execution sworn.

Pol.   I do believe thee:
I saw his heart in 's face.   Give me thy hand:
Be pilot to me and thy places shall
Still neighbour mine.   My ships are ready, and
My people did expect my hence departure   450
Two days ago.   This jealousy
Is for a precious creature: as she 's rare,
Must it be great; and, as his person 's mighty,
Must it be violent; and as he does conceive
He is dishonour'd by a man which ever
Profess'd to him, why, his revenges must
In that be made more bitter.   Fear o'ershades me:
Good expedition be my friend, and comfort
The gracious queen, part of his theme, but nothing
Of his ill-ta'en suspicion!   Come, Camillo;   460
I will respect thee as a father if
Thou bear'st my life off hence: let us avoid.
Cam. It is in mine authoity to command
The keys of all the posterns: please your highness
To take the urgent hour.   Come, sir away.
                              [*Exeunt.*

Play might be ✦ made out of
Polixenes Inchicton of Honour.

Act Second.

Scene I.

A room in Leontes' palace.

Enter Hermione, Mamillius, and Ladies.

Her. Take the boy to you: he so troubles me,
  'Tis past enduring.

First Lady. Come, my gracious lord,
  Shall I be your playfellow?

Mam.   No, I'll none of you.

First Lady. Why, my sweet lord?

Mam. You'll kiss me hard, and speak to me as if
  I were a baby still.   I love you better.

Sec. Lady. And why so, my lord?

Mam.   Not for because
  Your brows are blacker; yet black brows, they say,
  Become some women best, so that there be not
  Too much hair there, but in a semicircle,   10
  Or a half-moon made with a pen.

Sec. Lady.   Who taught you this!

Mam. I learn'd it out of women's faces.   Pray now
  What colour are your eyebrows?

First Lady.   Blue, my lord.

Mam. Nay, that's a mock : I have seen a lady's nose ~cheeky child !~
   That has been blue, but not her eyebrows.

First Lady.   Hark ye;
   The queen your mother rounds apace : we shall
   Present our services to a fine new prince
   One of these days ; and then you 'ld wanton with us,
   If we would have you.

Sec. Lady.   She is spread of late
   Into a goodly bulk : good time encounter her !   20

Her. What wisdom stirs amongst you?   Come, Sir, now
   I am for you again : pray you, sit by us,
   And tell 's a tale.

Mam.   Merry or sad shall 't be?

Her. As merry as you will.

Mam. A sad tale 's best for winter : I have one
   Of sprites and goblins.

Her.   Let's have that, good sir.
   Come on, sit down : come on, and do your best
   To fright me with your sprites ; you 're powerful
       at it.

Mam. There was a man—

Her.   Nay, come, sit down ; then on.

Mam. Dwelt by a churchyard : I will tell it softly ;   30
   Yond crickets shall not hear it.

Her.   Come on, then,

27

And give't me in mine ear.

Enter Leontes, with Antigonus, Lords, and others.

Leon. Was he met there? his train? Camillo with him?

First Lord. Behind the tuft of pines I met them; never
    Saw I men scour so on their way: I eyed them
    Even to their ships.

Leon.   How blest am I
    In my just censure, in my true opinion!
    Alack, for lesser knowledge! how accursed
    In being so blest! There may be in the cup
    A spider steep'd, and one may drink, depart,   40
    And yet partake no venom; for his knowledge
    Is not infected: but if one present
    The abhorr'd ingredient to his eye, make known
    How he hath drunk, he cracks his gorge, his sides,
    With violent hefts. I have drunk, and seen the spider.
    Camillo was his help in this, his pandar:
    There is a plot against my life, my crown;
    All's true that is mistrusted: that false villain
    Whom I employ'd was pre-employ'd by him:
    He has discover'd my design, and I   50
    Remain a pinch'd thing; yea, a very trick
    For them to play at will. How came the posterns
    So easily open?

First Lord.   By his great authority ;
    Which often hath no less prevail'd than so
    On your command.

Leon.   I know 't too well.
    Give me the boy : I am glad you did not nurse him :
    Though he does bear some signs of me, yet you
    Have too much blood in him.

Her.   What is this ? sport ?

Leon. Bear the boy hence ; he shall not come about her ;
    Away with him ! and let her sport herself   60
    With that she 's big with ; for 'tis Polixenes
    Has made the swell thus.

Her.   But I 'ld say he had not,
    And I 'll be sworn you would believe my saying,
    Howe'er you lean to the nayward.

Leon.   You, my lords,
    Look on her, mark her well ; be but about
    To say 'she is a goodly lady,' and
    The justice of your hearts will thereto add
    ' 'Tis pity she 's not honest, honourable : '
    Praise her but for this her without-door form,
    Which on my faith deserves high speech, and straight
    The shrug, the hum or ha, these pretty brands   71
    That calumny doth use ; O, I am out,
    That mercy does, for calumny will sear

Virtue itself: these shrugs, these hums and ha's,
When you have said 'she's goodly,' come between
Ere you can say 'she's honest:' but be't known,
From him that has most cause to grieve it should be,
She's an adulteress.

Her.   Should a villain say so,
The most replenish'd villain in the world,
He were as much more villain: you, my lord,   80
Do but mistake.

Leon.   You have mistook, my lady,
Polixenes for Leontes: O thou <u>thing</u>!
Which I'll not call a creature of thy place,
Lest barbarism, making me the precedent,
Should a like language use to all degrees,
And mannerly distinguishment leave out
Betwixt the prince and beggar: I have said
She's an adulteress; I have said with whom:
More, she's a traitor and Camillo is
A federary with her; and one that knows,   90
What she should shame to know herself
But with her most vile principal, that she's
A bed-swerver, even as bad as those
That vulgars give bold'st titles; ay, and privy
To this their late escape.

Her.   No, by my life,

Privy to none of this.   How will this grieve you,
When you shall come to clearer knowledge, that
You thus have publish'd me !   Gentle my lord,
You scarce can right me thoroughly then to say
You did mistake.

Leon.   No ; if I mistake   100
In those foundations which I build upon,
The centre is not big enough to bear
A school-boy's top.   Away with her, to prison !
He who shall speak for her is afar off guilty
But that he speaks.

Her.   There 's some ill planet reigns :
I must be patient till the heavens look
With an aspect more favourable.   Good my lords,
I am not prone to weeping, as our sex
Commonly are ; the want of which vain dew
Perchance shall dry your pities : but I have   110
That honourable grief lodged here which burns
Worse than tears drown : beseech you all, my lords,
With thoughts so qualified as your charities
Shall best instruct you, measure me ; and so
The king's will be perform'd !

Leon.   Shall I be heard ?

Her. Who is 't that goes with me ?   Beseech your high-
     ness,

My women may be with me; for you see
My plight requires it.   Do not weep, good fools;
There is no cause: when you shall know your
     mistress
Has deserved prison, then abound in tears   120
As I come out: this action I now go on
Is for my better grace.   Adieu, my lord:
I never wish'd to see you sorry; now
I trust I shall.   My women, come; you have leave.

Leon. Go, do our bidding; hence !

               [Exit Queen, guarded; with Ladies.

First Lord. Beseech your highness, call the queen again.

Ant. Be certain what you do, sir, lest your justice
Prove violence; in the which three great ones suffer,
Yourself, your queen, your son.

First Lord.   For her, my lord,
I dare my life lay down and will do 't, sir,   130
Please you to accept it, that the queen is spotless
I' the eyes of heaven and to you; I mean,
In this which you accuse her.

Ant.   If it prove
She 's otherwise, I 'll keep my stables where
I lodge my wife; I 'll go in couples with her;
Than when I feel and see her no farther trust her;
For every inch of woman in the world,

Ay, every dram of woman's flesh is false,
If she be.

Leon.   Hold your peaces.

First Lord.   Good my lord,—

Ant. It is for you we speak, not for ourselves: 140
You are abused, and by some putter-on
That will be damn'd for 't; would I knew the villain,
I would land-damn him. Be she honour-flaw'd,
I have three daughters; the eldest is eleven;
The second and the third, nine, and some five;
If this prove true, they 'll pay for 't: by mine honour,
I 'll geld 'em all; fourteen they shall not see,
To bring false generations: they are co-heirs;
And I had rather glib myself than they
Should not produce fair issue.

Leon.   Cease; no more.   150
You smell this business with a sense as cold
As is a dead man's nose: but I do see 't and feel 't,
As you feel doing thus; and see withal
The instruments that feel.

Ant.   If it be so,
We need no grave to bury honesty:
There 's not a grain of it the face to sweeten
Of the whole dungy earth.

Leon.   What ! lack I credit ?

First Lord. I had rather you did lack than I, my lord,
Upon this ground ; and more it would content me
To have her honour true than your suspicion,   160
Be blamed for 't how you might.

Leon.   Why, what need we
Commune with you of this, but rather follow
Our forceful instigation ?   Our prerogative
Calls not your counsels, but our natural goodness
Imparts this ; which if you, or stupified
Or seeming so in skill, cannot or will not
Relish a truth like us, inform yourselves
We need no more of your advice : the matter,
The loss, the gain, the ordering on 't, is all
Properly ours.

Ant.   And I wish, my liege,   170
You had only in your silent judgement tried it,
Without more overture.

Leon.   How could that be ?
Either thou art most ignorant by age,
Or thou wert born a fool.   Camillo's flight,
Added to their familiarity,
Which was as gross as ever touch'd conjecture,
That lack'd sight only, nought for approbation
But only seeing, all other circumstances
Made up to the deed,—doth push on this proceeding:

Yet, for a greater confirmation,   180
For in an act of this importance 'twere
Most piteous to be wild, I have dispatch'd in post
To sacred Delphos, to Apollo's temple,
Cleomenes and Dion, whom you know
Of stuff'd sufficiency : now from the oracle
They will bring all ; whose spiritual counsel had,
Shall stop or spur me.   Have I done well ?

First Lord.   Well done, my lord.

Leon. Though I am satisfied and need no more
Than what I know, yet shall the oracle   190
Give rest to the minds of others, such as he
Whose ignorant credulity will not
Come up to the truth.   So have we thought it good
From our free person she should be confined,
Lest that the treachery of the two fled hence
Be left her to perform.   Come, follow us ;
We are to speak in public ; for this business
Will raise us all.

Ant.   [*Aside*] To laughter, as I take it,
If the good truth were known.   [*Exeunt.*

Scene II.

A prison.

Enter Paulina, a Gentleman, and Attendants.

Paul. The keeper of the prison, call to him;
    Let him have knowledge who I am.   [*Exit Gent.*
                          Good lady,
    No court in Europe is too good for thee;
    What dost thou then in prison?

Re-enter Gentleman, with the Gaoler.

                        Now, good sir,
    You know me, do you not?
Gaol.   For a worthy lady
    And one who much I honour.
Paul.   Pray you, then,
    Conduct me to the queen.
Gaol.   I may not, madam:
    To the contrary I have express commandment.
Paul. Here's ado,
    To lock up honesty and honour from   10
    The access of gentle visitors! Is't lawful, pray you,
    To see her women? any of them? Emilia?

Gaol. So please you, madam,
  To put apart these your attendants, I
  Shall bring Emilia forth.
Paul.   I pray now, call her.
  Withdraw yourselves.

                [Exeunt Gentleman and Attendants.
Gaol.   And, madam,
  I must be present at your conference.
Paul. Well, be 't so, prithee.   *[Exit Gaoler.*
  Here 's such ado to make no stain a stain
  As passes colouring.

        Re-enter Gaoler, with Emilia.

                Dear gentlewoman,   20
  How fares our gracious lady?
Emil. As well as one so great and so forlorn
  May hold together : on her frights and griefs,
  Which never tender lady hath borne greater,
  She is something before her time deliver'd.
Paul. A boy?
Emil.   A daughter ; and a goodly babe,
  Lusty and like to live : the queen receives
  Much comfort in 't ; says 'My poor prisoner,
  I am innocent as you.'
Paul.   I dare be sworn :

These dangerous unsafe lunes i' the king, beshrew
    them !   30
He must be told on 't, and he shall : the office
Becomes a woman best ; I 'll take 't upon me :
If I prove honey-mouth'd, let my tongue blister,
And never to my red-look'd anger be
The trumpet any more.   Pray you, Emilia,
Commend my best obedience to the queen :
If she dares trust me with her little babe,
I 'll show 't the king and undertake to be
Her advocate to the loud'st.   We do not know
How he may soften at the sight o' the child :   40
The silence often of pure innocence
Persuades when speaking fails.

Emil.   Most worthy madam,
Your honour and your goodness is so evident,
That your free undertaking cannot miss
A thriving issue : there is no lady living
So meet for this great errand.   Please your ladyship
To visit the next room, I 'll presently
Acquaint the queen of your most noble offer ;
Who but to-day hammer'd of this design,
But durst not tempt a minister of honour,   50
Lest she should be denied.

Paul.   Tell her, Emilia,

      I 'll use that tongue I have : if wit flow from 't
      As boldness from my bosom, let 't not be doubted
      I shall do good.

Emil.   Now be you blest for it !
      I 'll to the queen : please you, come something nearer.

Gaol. Madam, if 't please the queen to send the babe,
      I know not what I shall incur to pass it,
      Having no warrant.

Paul.   You need not fear it, sir :
      This child was prisoner to the womb, and is
      By law and process of great nature thence   60
      Freed and enfranchised ; not a party to
      The anger of the king, nor guilty of,
      If any be, the trespass of the queen.

Gaol. I do believe it.

Paul. Do not you fear : upon mine honour, I
      Will stand betwixt you and danger.   [*Exeunt.*

Scene III.

A room in Leontes' palace.

Enter Leontes, Antigonus, Lords, and Servants.

Leon. Nor night nor day no rest : it is but weakness
      To bear the matter thus ; mere weakness. If

The cause were not in being,—part o' the cause,
She the adulteress; for the harlot king
Is quite beyond mine arm, out of the blank
And level of my brain, plot-proof; but she
I can hook to me: say that she were gone,
Given to the fire, a moiety of my rest
Might come to me again.   Who's there?

First Serv.   My lord!
Leon. How does the boy?
First Serv.   He took good rest to-night; 10
'Tis hoped his sickness is discharged.
Leon. To see his nobleness!
Conceiving the dishonour of his mother,
He straight declined, droop'd, took it deeply,
Fasten'd and fix'd the shame on 't in himself,
Threw off his spirit, his appetite, his sleep,
And downright languish'd.   Leave me solely: go,
See how he fares.   [*Exit Serv.*]   Fie, fie! no thought
    of him:
The very thought of my revenges that way
Recoil upon me: in himself too mighty,   20
And in his parties, his alliance; let him be
Until a time may serve: for present vengeance,
Take it on her.   Camillo and Polixenes
Laugh at me, make their pastime at my sorrow:

They should not laugh if I could reach them, nor
Shall she within my power.

Enter Paulina, with a child.

First Lord.   You must not enter.
Paul. Nay, rather, good my lords, be second to me :
     Fear you his tyrannous passion more, alas,
     Than the queen's life ? a gracious innocent soul.
     More free than he is jealous.
Ant.   That 's enough.   30
Sec. Serv. Madam, he hath not slept to-night ; com-
        manded
     None should come at him.
Paul.   Not so hot, good sir :
     I come to bring him sleep. 'Tis such as you,
     That creep like shadows by him, and do sigh
     At each his needless heavings, such as you
     Nourish the cause of his awaking : I
     Do come with words as medicinal as true,
     Honest as either, to purge him of that humour
     That presses him from sleep.
Leon.   What noise there, ho ?
Paul. No noise, my lord ; but needful conference   40
     About some gossips for your highness.
Leon.   How !

    Away with that audacious lady!　Antigonus,
    I charged thee that she should not come about me.
    I knew she would.

Ant.   I told her so, my lord,
    On your displeasure's peril and on mine,
    She should not visit you.

Leon.   What, canst not rule her?

Paul. From all dishonesty he can: in this,
    Unless he take the course that you have done,
    Commit me for committing honour, trust it,
    He shall not rule me.

Ant.   La you now, you hear: 50
    When she will take the rein I let her run;
    But she'll not stumble.

Paul.   Good my liege, I come;
    And, I beseech you, hear me, who professes
    Myself your loyal servant, your physician,
    Your most obedient counsellor, yet that dares
    Less appear so in comforting your evils,
    Than such as most seem yours: I say, I come
    From your good queen.

Leon.   Good queen!

Paul.   Good queen, my lord,
    Good queen; I say good queen;
    And would by combat make her good, so were I 60

A man, the worst about you.

Leon.   Force her hence.

Paul. Let him that makes but trifles of his eyes
First hand me: on mine own accord I'll off;
But first I'll do my errand.   The good queen,
For she is good, hath brought you forth a daughter;
Here 'tis; commends it to your blessing.

                              [*Laying down the child.*

Leon.   Out!

A mankind witch!   Hence with her, out o' door:
A most intelligencing bawd!

Paul.   Not so:

I am as ignorant in that as you
In so entitling me, and no less honest   70
Than you are mad; which is enough, I'll warrant,
As this world goes, to pass for honest.

Leon.   Traitors!

Will you not push her out?   Give her the bastard.
Thou dotard! thou art woman-tired, unroosted
By thy dame Partlet here.   Take up the bastard;
Take 't up, I say; give 't to thy crone.

Paul.   For ever

Unvenerable be thy hands, if thou
Takest up the princess by that forced baseness
Which he has put upon 't!

43

Leon.   He dreads his wife.

Paul. So I would you did; then 'twere past all doubt 80
   You'ld call your children yours.

Leon.   A nest of traitors!

Ant. I am none, by this good light.

Paul.   Nor I; nor any
   But one that's here, and that's himself; for he
   The sacred honour of himself, his queen's,
   His hopeful son's, his babe's, betrays to slander,
   Whose sting is sharper than the sword's; and will not,—
   For, as the case now stands, it is a curse
   He cannot be compell'd to 't,—once remove
   The root of his opinion, which is rotten
   As ever oak or stone was sound.

Leon.   A callat   90
   Of boundless tongue, who late hath beat her husband
   And now baits me!   This brat is none of mine;
   It is the issue of Polixenes:
   Hence with it, and together with the dam
   Commit them to the fire!

Paul.   It is yours;
   And, might we lay the old proverb to your charge,
   So like you, 'tis the worse.   Behold, my lords,
   Although the print be little, the whole matter
   And copy of the father, eye, nose, lip;   99

44

> The trick of 's frown; his forehead; nay, the valley,
> The pretty dimples of his chin and cheek; his smiles;
> The very mould and frame of hand, nail, finger:
> And thou, good goddess Nature, which hast made it
> So like to him that got it, if thou hast
> The ordering of the mind too, 'mongst all colours
> No yellow in 't, lest she suspect, as he does,
> Her children not her husband's!

Leon.   A gross hag!
> And, lozel, thou art worthy to be hang'd,
> That wilt not stay her tongue.

Ant.   Hang all the husbands 110
> That cannot do that feat, you'll leave yourself
> Hardly one subject.

Leon.   Once more, take her hence.

Paul. A most unworthy and unnatural lord
> Can do no more.

Leon.   I 'll ha' thee burnt.

Paul.   I care not:
> It is an heretic that makes the fire,
> Not she which burns in 't.   I 'll not call you tyrant;
> But this most cruel usage of your queen—
> Not able to produce more accusation
> Than your own weak-hinged fancy — something
> savours

Of tyranny, and will ignoble make you, 120
Yea, scandalous to the world.

Leon. On your allegiance,
Out of the chamber with her ! Were I a tyrant,
Where were her life ? she durst not call me so,
If she did know me one. Away with her !

Paul. I pray you, do not push me ; I'll be gone.
Look to your babe, my lord ; 'tis yours : Jove send her
A better guiding spirit ! What needs these hands ?
You, that are thus so tender o'er his follies,
Will never do him good, not one of you.
So, so : farewell ; we are gone. [*Exit.* 130

Leon. Thou, traitor, hast set on thy wife to this.
My child ? away with 't ! Even thou, that hast
A heart so tender o'er it, take it hence
And see it instantly consumed with fire ;
Even thou and none but thou. Take it up straight :
Within this hour bring me word 'tis done,
And by good testimony, or I'll seize thy life,
With what thou else call'st thine. If thou refuse
And wilt encounter with my wrath, say so ;
The bastard brains with these my proper hands
Shall I dash out. Go, take it to the fire ; 140
For thou set'st on thy wife.

Ant.   I did not, sir :
    These lords, my noble fellows, if they please,
    Can clear me in 't.

Lords.   We can ; my royal liege,
    He is not guilty of her coming hither.

Leon. You 're liars all.

First Lord. Beseech your highness, give us better credit :
    We have always truly served you ; and beseech you
    So to esteem of us : and on our knees we beg,
    As recompense of our dear services   150
    Past and to come, that you do change this purpose,
    Which being so horrible, so bloody, must
    Lead on to some foul issue : we all kneel.

Leon. I am a feather for each wind that blows :
    Shall I live on to see this bastard kneel
    And call me father ? better burn it now
    Than curse it then.   But be it ; let it live.
    It shall not neither.   You, sir, come you hither ;
    You that have been so tenderly officious
    With Lady Margery, your midwife there,   160
    To save this bastard's life,—for 'tis a bastard,
    So sure as this beard's grey,—what will you ad-
      venture
    To save this brat's life ?

Ant.   Any thing, my lord,

That my ability may undergo,
And nobleness impose : at least thus much.
I'll pawn the little blood which I have left
To save the innocent : any thing possible.

Leon. It shall be possible. Swear by this sword
Thou wilt perform my bidding.

Ant.   I will, my lord.

Leon. Mark and perform it : seest thou ? for the fail   170
Of any point in 't shall not only be
Death to thyself but to thy lewd-tongued wife,
Whom for this time we pardon. We enjoin thee,
As thou art liege-man to us, that thou carry
This female bastard hence, and that thou bear it
To some remote and desert place, quite out
Of our dominions ; and that there thou leave it,
Without more mercy, to it own protection
And favour of the climate. As by strange fortune
It came to us, I do in justice charge thee,   180
On thy soul's peril and thy body's torture,
That thou commend it strangely to some place
Where chance may nurse or end it. Take it up.

Ant. I swear to do this, though a present death
Had been more merciful. Come on, poor babe :
Some powerful spirit instruct the kites and ravens
To be thy nurses ! Wolves and bears, they say,

Casting their savageness aside have done
Like offices of pity.   Sir, be prosperous
In more than this deed does require!   And blessing
Against this cruelty fight on thy side,   191
Poor thing, condemn'd to loss! [*Exit with the child.*

Leon.   No, I 'll not rear
Another's issue.

            Enter a Servant.

Serv.   Please your highness, posts
From those you sent to the oracle are come
An hour since: Cleomenes and Dion,
Being well arrived from Delphos, are both landed,
Hasting to the court.

First Lord.   So please you, sir, their speed
Hath been beyond account.

Leon.   Twenty three days
They have been absent: 'tis good speed; foretells
The great Apollo suddenly will have   200
The truth of this appear.   Prepare you, lords;
Summon a session, that we may arraign
Our most disloyal lady; for, as she hath
Been publicly accused, so shall she have
A just and open trial.   While she lives
My heart will be a burthen to me.   Leave me,
And think upon my bidding.   [*Exeunt.*

Act Third.

Scene I.

A seaport in Sicilia.

Enter Cleomenes and Dion.

no real occasion for entrance [margin note]

Cleo. The climate's delicate, the air most sweet,
Fertile the isle, the temple much surpassing
The common praise it bears.

Dion.   I shall report,
For most it caught me, the celestial habits,
Methinks I so should term them, and the reverence
Of the grave wearers.   O, the sacrifice!
How ceremonious, solemn and unearthly
It was i' the offering!

Cleo.   But of all, the burst
And the ear-deafening voice o' the oracle,
Kin to Jove's thunder, so surprised my sense,   10
That I was nothing.

Dion.   If the event o' the journey
Prove as successful to the queen,—O be 't so!—
As it hath been to us rare, pleasant, speedy,
The time is worth the use on 't.

advantages of Italy! [margin note]

Cleo.   Great Apollo
    Turn all to the best! These proclamations,
    So forcing faults upon Hermione,
    I little like.
Dion.   The violent carriage of it
    Will clear or end the business: when the oracle,
    Thus by Apollo's great divine seal'd up,
    Shall the contents discover, something rare   20
    Even then will rush to knowledge. Go: fresh horses!
    And gracious be the issue.   [*Exeunt.*

                    Scene II.

                A court of Justice.

        Enter Leontes, Lords, and Officers.

Leon. This sessions, to our great grief we pronounce,
    Even pushes 'gainst our heart: the party tried
    The daughter of a king, our wife, and one
    Of us too much beloved.   Let us be clear'd
    Of being tyrannous, since we so openly
    Proceed in justice, which shall have due course,
    Even to the guilt or the purgation.
    Produce the prisoner.
Off. It is his highness' pleasure that the queen
    Appear in person here in court.   Silence!
                    51

Enter Hermione guarded ; Paulina and Ladies attending.

Leon. Read the indictment.

Off. [*reads*] Hermione, queen to the worthy
Leontes, king of Sicilia, thou art here accused
and arraigned of high treason, in committing
adultery with Polixenes, king of Bohemia, and
conspiring with Camillo to take away the life of
our sovereign lord the king, thy royal husband:
the pretence whereof being by circumstances
partly laid open, thou, Hermione, contrary to
the faith and allegiance of a true subject, didst   20
counsel and aid them, for their better safety, to
fly away by night.

Her. Since what I am to say must be but that
Which contradicts my accusation, and
The testimony on my part no other
But what comes from myself, it shall scarce boot me
To say 'not guilty:' mine integrity,
Being counted falsehood, shall, as I express it,
Be so received.   But thus, if powers divine
Behold our human actions, as they do,   30
I doubt not then but innocence shall make
False accusation blush, and tyranny
Tremble at patience.   You, my lord, best know,
Who least will seem to do so, my past life

Hath been as continent, as chaste, as true,
As I am now unhappy; which is more
Than history can pattern, though devised
And play'd to take spectators.   For behold me
A fellow of the royal bed, which owe
A moiety of the throne, a great king's daughter,   40
The mother to a hopeful prince, here standing
To prate and talk for life and honour 'fore
Who please to come and hear.   For life, I prize it
As I weigh grief, which I would spare: for honour,
'Tis a derivative from me to mine,
And only that I stand for.   I appeal
To your own conscience, sir, before Polixenes
Came to your court, how I was in your grace,
How merited to be so; since he came,
With what encounter so uncurrent I   50
Have strain'd, to appear thus: if one jot beyond
The bound of honour, or in act or will
That way inclining, harden'd be the hearts
Of all that hear me, and my near'st of kin
Cry fie upon my grave!

Leon.   I ne'er heard yet
That any of these bolder vices wanted
Less impudence to gainsay what they did
Than to perform it first.

Her.   That's true enough;
    Though 'tis a saying, sir, not due to me.
Leon. You will not own it.
Her.   More than mistress of   60
    Which comes to me in name of fault, I must not
    At all acknowledge.   For Polixenes,
    With whom I am accused, I do confess
    I loved him as in honour he required,
    With such a kind of love as might become
    A lady like me, with a love even such,
    So and no other, as yourself commanded :
    Which not to have done I think had been in me
    Both disobedience and ingratitude
    To you and toward your friend ; whose love had
            spoke,   70
    Even since it could speak, from an infant, freely
    That it was yours.   Now, for conspiracy,
    I know not how it tastes ; though it be dish'd
    For me to try how : all I know of it
    Is that Camillo was an honest man ;
    And why he left your court, the gods themselves,
    Wotting no more than I, are ignorant.
Leon. You knew of his departure, as you know
    What you have underta'en to do in 's absence.
Her. Sir,   80

54

    You speak a language that I understand not:
    My life stands in the level of your dreams,
    Which I'll lay down.

Leon.   Your actions are my dreams;
    You had a bastard by Polixenes,
    And I but dream'd it. As you were past all shame,—
    Those of your fact are so,—so past all truth:
    Which to deny concerns more than avails; for as
    Thy brat hath been cast out, like to itself,
    No father owning it,—which is, indeed,
    More criminal in thee than it,—so thou   90
    Shalt feel our justice, in whose easiest passage
    Look for no less than death.

Her.   Sir, spare your threats:
    The bug which you would fright me with I seek.
    To me can life be no commodity:
    The crown and comfort of my life, your favour,
    I do give lost; for I do feel it gone,
    But know not how it went. My second joy
    And first-fruits of my body, from his presence
    I am barr'd, like one infectious. My third comfort,
    Starr'd most unluckily, is from my breast,   100
    The innocent milk in its most innocent mouth,
    Haled out to murder: myself on every post
    Proclaim'd a strumpet: with immodest hatred

The child-bed privilege denied, which 'longs
To women of all fashion ; lastly, hurried
Here to this place, i' the open air, before
I have got strength of limit.   Now, my liege,
Tell me what blessings I have here alive,
That I should fear to die ?   Therefore proceed.
But yet hear this ; mistake me not ; no life,   110
I prize it not a straw, but for mine honour,
Which I would free, if I shall be condemn'd
Upon surmises, all proofs sleeping else
But what your jealousies awake, I tell you
'Tis rigour and not law.   Your honours all,
I do refer me to the oracle :
Apollo be my judge !

First Lord.   This your request
Is altogether just : therefore bring forth,
And in Apollo's name, his oracle.

> [*Exeunt certain Officers.*

Her. The Emperor of Russia was my father :   120
O that he were alive, and here beholding
His daughter's trial ! that he did but see
The flatness of my misery, yet with eyes
Of pity, not revenge !

> *Re-enter Officers, with Cleomenes and Dion.*

Off. You here shall swear upon this sword of justice,

That you, Cleomenes and Dion, have
Been both at Delphos, and from thence have brought
This seal'd-up oracle, by the hand deliver'd
Of great Apollo's priest, and that since then
You have not dared to break the holy seal   130
Nor read the secrets in 't.

Cleo. Dion.   All this we swear.

Leon. Break up the seals and read.

Off. [*reads*] Hermione is chaste; Polixenes blameless; Camillo a true subject; Leontes a jealous
tyrant; his innocent babe truly begotten; and
the king shall live without an heir, if that which
is lost be not found.

Lords. Now blessed be the great Apollo!

Her.   Praised!

Leon. Hast thou read truth?

Off.   Ay, my lord; even so
As it is here set down.   140

Leon. There is no truth at all i' the oracle:
The sessions shall proceed: this is mere falsehood.

Enter Servant.

Serv. My lord the king, the king!

Leon.   What is the business?

Serv. O sir, I shall be hated to report it!

The prince your son, with mere conceit and fear
Of the queen's speed, is gone.

Leon. How! gone!

Serv. Is dead.

Leon. Apollo 's angry; and the heavens themselves
Do strike at my injustice.　[*Hermione faints.*]
How now there!

Paul. This news is mortal to the queen: look down
And see what death is doing.

Leon. Take her hence: 150
Her heart is but o'ercharged; she will recover:
I have too much believed mine own suspicion:
Beseech you, tenderly apply to her
Some remedies for life.

　　[*Exeunt Paulina and Ladies, with Hermione.*
　　　　　Apollo, pardon
My great profaneness 'gainst thine oracle!
I 'll reconcile me to Polixenes;
New woo my queen; recall the good Camillo,
Whom I proclaim a man of truth, of mercy;
For, being transported by my jealousies
To bloody thoughts and to revenge, I chose 160
Camillo for the minister to poison
My friend Polixenes: which had been done,
But that the good mind of Camillo tardied

58

My swift command, though I with death and with
Reward did threaten and encourage him,
Not doing it and being done : he, most humane
And fill'd with honour, to my kingly guest
Unclasp'd my practice, quit his fortunes here,
Which you knew great, and to the hazard
Of all incertainties himself commended,   170
No richer than his honour : how he glisters
Thorough my rust ! and how his piety
Does my deeds make the blacker !

Re-enter Paulina.

Paul.   Woe the while !
   O, cut my lace, lest my heart, cracking it,
   Break too !

First Lord.   What fit is this, good lady ?

Paul. What studied torments, tyrant, hast for me ?
   What wheels ? racks ? fires ? what flaying ? boiling
   In leads or oils ? what old or newer torture
   Must I receive, whose every word deserves
   To taste of thy most worst ? Thy tyranny   180
   Together working with thy jealousies,
   Fancies too weak for boys, too green and idle
   For girls of nine, O, think what they have done
   And then run mad indeed, stark mad ! for all

Thy by-gone fooleries were but spices of it.
That thou betray'dst Polixenes, 'twas nothing;
That did but show thee, of a fool, inconstant
And damnable ingrateful: nor was 't much,
Thou wouldst have poison'd good Camillo's honour,
To have him kill a king; poor trespasses,   190
More monstrous standing by: whereof I reckon
The casting forth to crows thy baby-daughter
To be or none or little; though a devil
Would have shed water out of fire ere done 't:
Nor is 't directly laid to thee, the death
Of the young prince, whose honourable thoughts,
Thoughts high for one so tender, cleft the heart
That could conceive a gross and foolish sire
Blemish'd his gracious dam: this is not, no,
Laid to thy answer: but the last,—O lords,   200
When I have said, cry 'woe!'—the queen, the queen,
The sweet'st, dear'st creature 's dead, and vengeance
          for 't
Not dropp'd down yet.
First Lord.   The higher powers forbid!
Paul. I say she 's dead, I 'll swear 't. If word nor oath
Prevail not, go and see: if you can bring
Tincture or lustre in her lip, her eye,
Heat outwardly or breath within, I 'll serve you

As I would do the gods.   But, O thou tyrant!
Do not repent these things, for they are heavier
Than all thy woes can stir: therefore betake thee
To nothing but despair.   A thousand knees   211
Ten thousand years together, naked, fasting,
Upon a barren mountain, and still winter
In storm perpetual, could not move the gods
To look that way thou wert.

Leon.   Go on, go on:
Thou canst not speak too much; I have deserved
All tongues to talk their bitterest.

First Lord.   Say no more:
Howe'er the business goes, you have made fault
I' the boldness of your speech.

Paul.   I am sorry for 't:
All faults I make, when I shall come to know them,
I do repent.   Alas! I show'd too much   221
The rashness of a woman: he is touch'd
To the noble heart.   What 's gone and what 's past
      help
Should be past grief: do not receive affliction
At my petition; I beseech you, rather
Let me be punish'd, that have minded you
Of what you should forget.   Now, good my liege,
Sir, royal sir, forgive a foolish woman:

The love I bore your queen, lo, fool again!
I'll speak of her no more, nor of your children;
I'll not remember you of my own lord,　　231
Who is lost too: take your patience to you,
And I'll say nothing.

Leon.　　　　　　Thou didst speak but well
When most the truth; which I receive much better
Than to be pitied of thee.　Prithee, bring me
To the dead bodies of my queen and son:
One grave shall be for both; upon them shall
The causes of their death appear, unto
Our shame perpetual.　Once a day I'll visit
The chapel where they lie, and tears shed there 240
Shall be my recreation: so long as nature
Will bear up with this exercise, so long
I daily vow to use it.　Come and lead me
To these sorrows.　　　　　　　　　*[Exeunt.*

Scene III.

Bohemia.　A desert country near the sea.

Enter Antigonus with a Child, and a Mariner.

Ant. Thou are perfect, then, our ship hath touch'd upon
　　The deserts of Bohemia?

Mar.　　　　　　　　Ay, my lord; and fear

We have landed in ill time: the skies look grimly
And threaten present blusters.   In my conscience,
The heavens with that we have in hand are angry
And frown upon 's.

Ant. Their sacred wills be done!   Go, get aboard;
Look to thy bark: I 'll not be long before
I call upon thee.

Mar. Make your best haste, and go not   10
Too far i' the land: 'tis like to be loud weather;
Besides, this place is famous for the creatures
Of prey that keep upon 't.

Ant.   Go thou away:
I 'll follow instantly.

Mar.   I am glad at heart
To be so rid o' the business.   [*Exit.*

Ant.   Come, poor babe:
I have heard, but not believed, the spirits o' the dead
May walk again: if such thing be, thy mother
Appear'd to me last night, for ne'er was dream
So like a waking.   To me comes a creature,
Sometimes her head on one side, some another;   20
I never saw a vessel of like sorrow,
So fill'd and so becoming: in pure white robes,
Like very sanctity, she did approach
My cabin where I lay; thrice bow'd before me,

And, gasping to begin some speech, her eyes
Became two spouts : the fury spent, anon
Did this break from her : 'Good Antigonus,
Since fate, against thy better disposition,
Hath made thy person for the thrower-out
Of my poor babe, according to thine oath,　　　　　30
Places remote enough are in Bohemia,
There weep and leave it crying ; and, for the babe
Is counted lost for ever, Perdita,
I prithee, call 't.　For this ungentle business,
Put on thee by my lord, thou ne'er shalt see
Thy wife Paulina more.'　And so, with shrieks,
She melted into air.　Affrighted much,
I did in time collect myself, and thought
This was so, and no slumber.　Dreams are toys :
Yet for this once, yea, superstitiously,　　　　　40
I will be squared by this.　I do believe
Hermione hath suffer'd death ; and that
Apollo would, this being indeed the issue
Of King Polixenes, it should here be laid,
Either for life or death, upon the earth
Of its right father.　Blossom, speed thee well !
There lie, and there thy character : there these ;
Which may, if fortune please, both breed thee
　　　pretty,

And still rest thine.   The storm begins : poor wretch,
That for thy mother's fault art thus exposed   50
To loss and what may follow !   Weep I cannot,
But my heart bleeds ; and most accursed am I
To be by oath enjoin'd to this.   Farewell !
The day frowns more and more : thou 'rt like to have
A lullaby too rough : I never saw
The heavens so dim by day.   A savage clamour !
Well may I get aboard !   This is the chase :
I am gone for ever.   [*Exit, pursued by a bear*.

Enter a Shepherd.

Shep. I would there were no age between ten and
three-and-twenty, or that youth would sleep   60
out the rest ; for there is nothing in the between but getting wenches with child, wrong-
ing the ancientry, stealing, fighting—Hark you
now !   Would any but these boiled brains of
nineteen and two-and-twenty hunt this weather ?
They have scared away two of my best sheep,
which I fear the wolf will sooner find than the
master : if any where I have them, 'tis by the
sea-side, browzing of ivy.   Good luck, an 't be
thy will ! what have we here ?   Mercy on 's,   70

a barne ; very pretty barne ! A boy or a child,
I wonder ? A pretty one ; a very pretty one :
sure, some scape : though I am not bookish, yet
I can read waiting-gentlewoman in the scape.
This has been some stair-work, some trunk-
work, some behind-door-work: they were warmer
that got this than the poor thing is here. I 'll
take it up for pity: yet I 'll tarry till my son come;
he hallooed but even now. Whoa, ho, hoa !

Enter Clown.

Clo. Hilloa, loa ! 　　　　　　　　　　　　　　80
Shep. What, art so near ? If thou 'lt see a thing to
　　talk on when thou art dead and rotten, come
　　hither. What ailest thou, man ?
Clo. I have seen two such sights, by sea and by
　　land ! but I am not to say it is a sea, for it is
　　now the sky : betwixt the firmament and it you
　　cannot thrust a bodkin's point.
Shep. Why, boy, how is it ?
Clo. I would you did but see how it chafes, how
　　it rages, how it takes up the shore ! but that 's　　90
　　not to the point. O, the most piteous cry of
　　the poor souls ! sometimes to see 'em, and not
　　to see 'em ; now the ship boring the moon with

her main-mast, and anon swallowed with yest
and froth, as you 'ld thrust a cork into a hogs-
head. And then for the land service, to see
how the bear tore out his shoulder-bone; how
he cried to me for help and said his name was
Antigonus, a nobleman. But to make an end
of the ship, to see how the sea flap-dragoned it : 100
but, first, how the poor souls roared, and the
sea mocked them; and how the poor gentleman roared and the bear mocked him, both
roaring louder than the sea or weather.

Shep. Name of mercy, when was this, boy?

Clo. Now, now: I have not winked since I saw
these sights: the men are not yet cold under
water, nor the bear half dined on the gentleman: he 's at it now.

Shep. Would I had been by, to have helped the 110
old man!

Clo. I would you had been by the ship side, to have
helped her: there your charity would have
lacked footing.

Shep. Heavy matters! heavy matters! but look
thee here, boy. Now bless thyself: thou
mettest with things dying, I with things new-
born. Here 's a sight for thee; look thee, a

bearing-cloth for a squire's child! look thee here; take up, take up, boy; open 't. So, 120 let 's see: it was told me I should be rich by the fairies. This is some changeling: open 't. What 's within, boy?

Clo. You're a made old man: if the sins of your youth are forgiven you, you 're well to live. Gold! all gold!

Shep. This is fairy gold, boy, and 'twill prove so: up with 't, keep it close: home, home, the next way. We are lucky, boy; and to be so still requires nothing but secrecy. Let my sheep 130 go: come, good boy, the next way home.

Clo. Go you the next way with your findings. I'll go see if the bear be gone from the gentleman and how much he hath eaten: they are never curst but when they are hungry: if there be any of him left, I'll bury it.

Shep. That's a good deed. If thou mayest discern by that which is left of him what he is, fetch me to the sight of him.

Clo. Marry, will I; and you shall help to put him 140 i' the ground.

Shep. 'Tis a lucky day, boy, and we'll do good deeds on 't. [*Exeunt.*

Act Fourth.

Scene I.

Enter Time, the Chorus.

Time. I, that please some, try all, both joy and terror
   Of good and bad, that makes and unfolds error,
   Now take upon me, in the name of Time,
   To use my wings. Impute it not a crime
   To me or my swift passage, that I slide
   O'er sixteen years and leave the growth untried
   Of that wide gap, since it is in my power
   To o'erthrow law and in one self-born hour
   To plant and o'erwhelm custom. Let me pass
   The same I am, ere ancient'st order was   **10**
   Or what is now received: I witness to
   The times that brought them in; so shall I do
   To the freshest things now reigning, and make stale
   The glistering of this present, as my tale
   Now seems to it. Your patience this allowing,
   I turn my glass and give my scene such growing
   As you had slept between: Leontes leaving,
   The effects of his fond jealousies so grieving

That he shuts up himself, imagine me,
Gentle spectators, that I now may be   20
In fair Bohemia; and remember well,
I mentioned a son o' the king's, which Florizel
I now name to you; and with speed so pace
To speak of Perdita, now grown in grace
Equal with wondering: what of her ensues
I list not prophesy; but let Time's news
Be known when 'tis brought forth.   A shepherd's
     daughter,
And what to her adheres, which follows after,
Is the argument of Time.   Of this allow,
If ever you have spent time worse ere now;   30
If never, yet that Time himself doth say
He wishes earnestly you never may.   [*Exit.*

Scene II.

Bohemia.   The palace of Polixenes.

Enter Polixenes and Camillo.

Pol. I pray thee, good Camillo, be no more impor-
     tunate: 'tis a sickness denying thee any thing;
     a death to grant this.

Cam. It is fifteen years since I saw my country:

though I have for the most part been aired abroad, I desire to lay my bones there. Besides, the penitent king, my master, hath sent for me; to whose feeling sorrows I might be some allay, or I o'erween to think so, which is another spur to my departure.   10

Pol. As thou lovest me, Camillo, wipe not out the rest of thy services by leaving me now: the need I have of thee, thine own goodness hath made; better not to have had thee than thus to want thee: thou, having made me businesses, which none without thee can sufficiently manage, must either stay to execute them thyself, or take away with thee the very services thou hast done; which if I have not enough considered, as too much I cannot, to be more thankful to thee shall   20 be my study; and my profit therein, the heaping friendships. Of that fatal country, Sicilia, prithee speak no more; whose very naming punishes me with the remembrance of that penitent, as thou callest him, and reconciled king, my brother; whose loss of his most precious queen and children are even now to be afresh lamented. Say to me, when sawest thou the **Prince Florizel**, my son? Kings are no less

unhappy, their issue not being gracious, than   30
they are in losing them when they have
approved their virtues.

Cam. Sir, it is three days since I saw the prince.
What his happier affairs may be, are to me
unknown: but I have missingly noted, he is of
late much retired from court and is less frequent
to his princely exercises than formerly he hath
appeared.

Pol. I have considered so much, Camillo, and with
some care; so far, that I have eyes under my   40
service which look upon his removedness; from
whom I have this intelligence, that he is seldom
from the house of a most homely shepherd; a
man, they say, that from very nothing, and
beyond the imagination of his neighbours, is
grown into an unspeakable estate.

Cam. I have heard, sir, of such a man, who hath a
daughter of most rare note: the report of her
is extended more than can be thought to begin
from such a cottage.   50

Pol. That's likewise part of my intelligence; but,
I fear, the angle that plucks our son thither.
Thou shalt accompany us to the place; where
we will, not appearing what we are, have some

question with the shepherd; from whose sim-
plicity I think it not uneasy to get the cause
of my son's resort thither. Prithee, be my
present partner in this business, and lay aside
the thoughts of Sicilia.

Cam. I willingly obey your command.   60

Pol. My best Camillo! We must disguise ourselves.   [*Exeunt.*

Scene III.

A road near the Shepherd's cottage.

Enter Autolycus, singing.

When daffodils begin to peer,
    With heigh! the doxy over the dale,
Why, then comes in the sweet o' the year;
    For the red blood reigns in the winter's pale.

The white sheet bleaching on the hedge,
    With heigh! the sweet birds, O, how they sing!
Doth set my pugging tooth on edge;
    For a quart of ale is a dish for a king.

The lark, that tirra-lyra chants,
   With heigh! with heigh! the thrush and the jay,
Are summer songs for me and my aunts,   **11**
   While we lie tumbling in the hay.

I have served Prince Florizel and in my time
wore three-pile; but now I am out of service:

But shall I go mourn for that, my dear?
   The pale moon shines by night:
And when I wander here and there,
   I then do most go right.

If tinkers may have leave to live,
   And bear the sow-skin budget,
Then my account I well may give,   **20**
   And in the stocks avouch it.

My traffic is sheets; when the kite builds, look
to lesser linen. My father named me Autolycus;
who being, as I am, littered under Mercury, was
likewise a snapper-up of unconsidered trifles.
With die and drab I purchased this caparison,
and my revenue is the silly cheat. Gallows and
knock are too powerful on the highway: beat-

ing and hanging are terrors to me: for the life   30
to come, I sleep out the thought of it. A prize!
a prize!

Enter Clown.

Clo. Let me see: every 'leven wether tods; every
tod yields pound and odd shilling; fifteen hun-
dred shorn, what comes the wool to?

Aut. [*Aside*] If the springe hold, the cock's
mine.

Clo. I cannot do 't without counters. Let me see;
what am I to buy for our sheep-shearing feast?
Three pound of sugar; five pound of currants;   40
rice—what will this sister of mine do with rice?
But my father hath made her mistress of the
feast, and she lays it on. She hath made me
four and twenty nosegays for the shearers, three-
man song-men all, and very good ones; but they
are most of them means and bases; but one puritan amongst them, and he sings psalms to hornpipes. I must have saffron to colour the warden
pies; mace; dates, none, that's out of my note;
nutmegs, seven; a race or two of ginger, but   50
that I may beg; four pound of prunes, and as
many of raisins o' the sun.

Aut. O that ever I was born! [*Grovelling on the ground.*

Clo. I' the name of me—

Aut. O, help me, help me! pluck but off these rags; and then, death, death!

Clo. Alack, poor soul! thou hast need of more rags to lay on thee, rather than have these off.

Aut. O sir, the loathsomeness of them offends me more than the stripes I have received, which are 60 mighty ones and millions.

Clo. Alas, poor man! a million of beating may come to a great matter.

Aut. I am robbed, sir, and beaten; my money and apparel ta'en from me, and these detestable things put upon me.

Clo. What, by a horseman, or a footman?

Aut. A footman, sweet sir, a footman.

Clo. Indeed, he should be a footman by the garments he has left with thee: if this be a horseman's 70 coat, it hath seen very hot service. Lend me thy hand, I'll help thee: come, lend me thy hand.   [*Helping him up.*

Aut. O, good sir, tenderly, O!

Clo. Alas, poor soul!

Aut. O, good sir, softly, good sir! I fear, sir, my shoulder-blade is out.

76

Clo. How now! canst stand?

Aut. Softly, dear sir [*picks his pocket*]; good sir, softly. You ha' done me a charitable 80 office.

Clo. Dost lack any money? I have a little money for thee.

Aut. No, good sweet sir; no, I beseech you, sir: I have a kinsman not past three quarters of a mile hence, unto whom I was going; I shall there have money, or any thing I want: offer me no money, I pray you; that kills my heart.

Clo. What manner of fellow was he that robbed you? 90

Aut. A fellow, sir, that I have known to go about with troll-my-dames: I knew him once a servant of the prince: I cannot tell, good sir, for which of his virtues it was, but he was certainly whipped out of the court.

Clo. His vices, you would say; there's no virtue whipped out of the court: they cherish it to make it stay there; and yet it will no more but abide.

Aut. Vices I would say, sir. I know this man 100 well: he hath been since an ape-bearer; then a process-server, a bailiff; then he compassed a

motion of the Prodigal Son, and married a tin-
ker's wife within a mile where my land and
living lies; and, having flown over many
knavish professions, he settled only in rogue:
some call him Autolycus.

Clo. Out upon him! prig, for my life, prig: he
haunts wakes, fairs and bear-baitings.

Aut. Very true, sir; he, sir, he; that's the rogue 110
that put me into this apparel.

Clo. Not a more cowardly rogue in all Bohemia:
if you had but looked big and spit at him, he'ld
have run.

Aut. I must confess to you, sir, I am no fighter:
I am false of heart that way; and that he
knew, I warrant him.

Clo. How do you now?

Aut. Sweet sir, much better than I was; I can stand
and walk: I will even take my leave of you, 120
and pace softly towards my kinsman's.

Clo. Shall I bring thee on the way?

Aut. No, good-faced sir; no, sweet sir.

Clo. Then fare thee well: I must go buy spices for
our sheep-shearing.

Aut. Prosper you, sweet sir! [*Exit Clown.*]
Your purse is not hot enough to purchase your

spice.   I 'll be with you at your sheep-shearing
too : if I make not this cheat bring out another
and the shearers prove sheep, let me be unrolled 130
and my name put in the book of virtue !

Song.   Jog on, jog on, the foot-path way,
         And merrily hent the stile-a :
     A merry heart goes all the day,
         Your sad tires in a mile-a.   [*Exit.*

Scene IV.

The Shepherd's cottage.

Enter Florizel and Perdita.

Flo.   These your unusual weeds to each part of you
Do give a life : no shepherdess, but Flora
Peering in April's front.   This your sheep-shearing
Is as a meeting of the petty gods,
And you the queen on 't.

Per.   Sir, my gracious lord,
To chide at your extremes it not becomes me :
O, pardon, that I name them !   Your high self,
The gracious mark o' the land, you have obscured
With a swain's wearing, and me, poor lowly maid,

Most goddess-like prank'd up: but that our feasts
In every mess have folly and the feeders   11
Digest it with a custom, I should blush ~~tremblable~~
To see you so attired, sworn, I think,
To show myself a glass.

course of a feast.

Flo.   I bless the time
When my good falcon made her flight across
Thy father's ground.

Per.   Now Jove afford you cause!
To me the difference forges dread; your greatness
Hath not been used to fear.   Even now I tremble
To think your father, by some accident,
Should pass this way as you did: O, the Fates! 20
How would he look, to see his work, so noble,
Vilely bound up?   What would he say?   Or how
Should I, in these my borrow'd flaunts, behold
The sternness of his presence?

Flo.   Apprehend
Nothing but jollity.   The gods themselves,
Humbling their deities to love, have taken
The shapes of beasts upon them: Jupiter
Became a bull, and bellow'd; the green Neptune
A ram, and bleated; and the fire-robed god,
Golden Apollo, a poor humble swain,   30
As I seem now.   Their transformations

Were never for a piece of beauty rarer,
Nor in a way so chaste, since my desires
Run not before mine honour, nor my lusts
Burn hotter than my faith.

Per.   O, but, sir,
Your resolution cannot hold, when 'tis
Opposed, as it must be, by the power of the king:
One of these two must be necessities,
Which then will speak, that you must change this
       purpose,
Or I my life.

Flo.   Thou dearest Perdita,   40
With these forced thoughts, I prithee, darken not
The mirth o' the feast. Or I'll be thine, my fair,
Or not my father's. For I cannot be
Mine own, nor any thing to any, if
I be not thine. To this I am most constant,
Though destiny say no. Be merry, gentle;
Strangle such thoughts as these with any thing
That you behold the while. Your guests are coming:
Lift up your countenance, as it were the day
Of celebration of that nuptial which   50
We two have sworn shall come.

Per.   O lady Fortune,
Stand you auspicious!

           8x

Flo.　　　　　　　See, your guests approach:
Address yourself to entertain them sprightly,
And let 's be red with mirth.

Enter Shepherd, Clown, Mopsa, Dorcas, and others, with
Polixenes and Camillo disguised.

Shep. Fie, daughter! when my old wife lived, upon
This day she was both pantler, butler, cook,
Both dame and servant; welcomed all, served all:
Would sing her song and dance her turn; now here,
At upper end o' the table, now i' the middle;
On his shoulder, and his; her face o' fire　　　 60
With labour and the thing she took to quench it,
She would to each one sip.　You are retired,
As if you were a feasted one and not
The hostess of the meeting: pray you, bid
These unknown friends to 's welcome; for it is
A way to make us better friends, more known.
Come, quench your blushes and present yourself
That which you are, mistress o' the feast: come on,
And bid us welcome to your sheep-shearing,
As your good flock shall prosper.
Per.　　　　　　　[*To Pol.*] Sir, welcome:　70
It is my father's will I should take on me

The hostess-ship o' the day. [*To Cam.*] You 're
    welcome, sir.
Give me those flowers there, Dorcas. Reverend sirs,
For you there 's rosemary and rue; these keep
Seeming and savour all the winter long:
Grace and remembrance be to you both,
And welcome to our shearing!

Pol.   Shepherdess,
A fair one are you, well you fit our ages
With flowers of winter.

Per.   Sir, the year growing ancient,
Not yet on summer's death, nor on the birth   80
Of trembling winter, the fairest flowers o' the season
Are our carnations and streak'd gillyvors,
Which some call nature's bastards: of that kind
Our rustic garden 's barren; and I care not
To get slips of them.

Pol.   Wherefore, gentle maiden,
Do you neglect them?

Per.   For I have heard it said
There is an art which in their piedness shares
With great creating nature.

Pol.   Say there be;
Yet nature is made better by no mean,
But nature makes that mean: so, over that art   90

Which you say adds to nature, is an art
That nature makes.   You see, sweet maid, we marry
A gentler scion to the wildest stock,
And make conceive a bark of baser kind
By bud of nobler race : this is an art
Which does mend nature, change it rather, but
The art itself is nature.

Per.   So it is.
Pol. Then make your garden rich in gillyvors,
  And do not call them bastards.

Per.   I 'll not put
The dibble in earth to set one slip of them ;   100
No more than were I painted I would wish
This youth should say 'twere well, and only therefore
Desire to breed by me.   Here 's flowers for you ;
Hot lavender, mints, savory, marjoram ;
The marigold, that goes to bed wi' the sun
And with him rises weeping : these are flowers
Of middle summer, and I think they are given
To men of middle age.   You're very welcome.
Cam. I should leave grazing, were I of your flock
  And only live by grazing.

Per.   Out, alas !   110
You 'ld be so lean, that blasts of January
Would blow you through and through.   Now, my
        fair'st friend.   84

I would I had some flowers o' the spring that might
Become your time of day; and yours, and yours,
That wear upon your virgin branches yet
Your maidenheads growing: O Proserpina,
For the flowers now, that frighted thou let'st fall
From Dis's waggon! daffodils,
That come before the swallow dares, and take
The winds of March with beauty; violets dim, 120
But sweeter than the lids of Juno's eyes
Or Cytherea's breath; pale primroses,
That die unmarried, ere they can behold
Bright Phœbus in his strength, a malady
Most incident to maids; bold oxlips and
The crown imperial; lilies of all kinds,
The flower-de-luce being one! O, these I lack,
To make you garlands of; and my sweet friend,
To strew him o'er and o'er!

Flo.   What, like a corse?

Per. No, like a bank for love to lie and play on;   130
Not like a corse; or if, not to be buried,
But quick and in mine arms. Come, take your
            flowers:
Methinks I play as I have seen them do
In Whitsun pastorals: sure this robe of mine
Does change my disposition.

Flo.   What you do
        Still betters what is done.   When you speak, sweet,
        I 'ld have you do it ever: when you sing,
        I 'ld have you buy and sell so, so give alms,
        Pray so; and, for the ordering your affairs,
        To sing them too: when you do dance, I wish you
        A wave o' the sea, that you might ever do   141
        Nothing but that; move still, still so,
        And own no other function: each your doing,
        So singular in each particular,
        Crowns what you are doing in the present deeds,
        That all your acts are queens.

Per.   O Doricles,
        Your praises are too large: but that your youth,
        And the true blood which peeps fairly through 't,
        Do plainly give you out an unstain'd shepherd,
        With wisdom I might fear, my Doricles,   150
        You woo'd me the false way.

Flo.   I think you have
        As little skill to fear as I have purpose
        To put you to 't.   But come; our dance, I pray:
        Your hand, my Perdita: so turtles pair,
        That never mean to part.

Per.   I 'll swear for 'em.

Pol. This is the prettiest low-born lass that ever

Ran on the green-sward: nothing she does or seems
But smacks of something greater than herself,
Too noble for this place.

Cam.   He tells her something
That makes her blood look out: good sooth, she is
The queen of curds and cream.   161

Clo.   Come on, strike up!

Dor. Mopsa must be your mistress: marry, garlic,
To mend her kissing with!

Mop.   Now, in good time!

Clo. Not a word, a word, we stand upon our manners.
Come, strike up!

  [*Music. Here a dance of Shepherds and Shepherdesses.*

Pol. Pray, good shepherd, what fair swain is this
Which dances with your daughter?

Shep. They call him Doricles; and boasts himself
To have a worthy feeding: but I have it
Upon his own report and I believe it;   170
He looks like sooth. He says he loves my daughter:
I think so too; for never gazed the moon
Upon the water, as he 'll stand and read
As 'twere my daughter's eyes: and, to be plain,
I think there is not half a kiss to choose
Who loves another best.

Pol.   She dances featly.

Shep. So she does any thing ; though I report it,
That should be silent : if young Doricles
Do light upon her, she shall bring him that
Which he not dreams of. 180

Enter Servant.

Serv. O master, if you did but hear the pedlar at
the door, you would never dance again after a
tabor and pipe ; no, the bagpipe could not move
you : he sings several tunes faster than you'll
tell money ; he utters them as he had eaten
ballads and all men's ears grew to his tunes.

Clo. He could never come better ; he shall come in.
I love a ballad but even too well, if it be doleful matter merrily set down, or a very pleasant
thing indeed and sung lamentably. 190

Serv. He hath songs for man or woman, of all sizes ;
no milliner can so fit his customers with gloves :
he has the prettiest love-songs for maids ; so
without bawdry, which is strange ; with such
delicate burthens of dildos and fadings, 'jump
her and thump her ; ' and where some stretch-
mouthed rascal would, as it were, mean mischief
and break a foul gap into the matter, he makes
the maid to answer ' Whoop, do me no harm,

good man;' puts him off, slights him, with 200
'Whoop, do me no harm, good man.'

Pol. This is a brave fellow.

Clo. Believe me, thou talkest of an admirable con-
ceited fellow. Has he any unbraided wares?

Serv. He hath ribbons of all the colours i' the
rainbow; points more than all the lawyers in
Bohemia can learnedly handle, though they
come to him by the gross: inkles, caddisses,
cambrics, lawns: why, he sings 'em over as
they were gods or goddesses; you would think 210
a smock were a she-angel, he so chants to the
sleeve-hand and the work about the square on 't.

Clo. Prithee bring him in; and let him approach
singing.

Per. Forewarn him that he use no scurrilous words
in 's tunes.   [*Exit Servant.*

Clo. You have of these pedlars, that have more in
them than you 'ld think, sister.

Per. Ay, good brother, or go about to think.

Enter Autolycus, singing.

Lawn as white as driven snow;   220
Cypress black as e'er was crow;

Gloves as sweet as damask roses;
Masks for faces and for noses;
Bugle bracelet, necklace amber,
Perfume for a lady's chamber;
Golden quoifs and stomachers,
For my lads to give their dears;
Pins and poking-sticks of steel,
What maids lack from head to heel:
Come buy of me, come; come buy, come buy;
Buy, lads, or else your lasses cry   231
Come buy.

Clo. If I were not in love with Mopsa, thou shouldst take no money of me; but being enthralled as I am, it will also be the bondage of certain ribbons and gloves.

Mop. I was promised them against the feast; but they come not too late now.

Dor. He hath promised you more than that, or there be liars.   240

Mop. He hath paid you all he promised you: may be, he has paid you more, which will shame you to give him again.

Clo. Is there no manners left among maids? will they wear their plackets where they should bear

their faces?   Is there not milking-time, when
you are going to bed, or kiln-hole, to whistle
off these secrets, but you must be title-tatt-
ling before all our guests? 'tis well they are
whispering: clamour your tongues, and not a 250
word more.

Mop. I have done. Come, you promised me a
tawdry-lace and a pair of sweet gloves.

Clo. Have I not told thee how I was cozened by
the way and lost all my money?

Aut. And indeed, sir, there are cozeners abroad;
therefore it behoves men to be wary.

Clo. Fear not thou, man, thou shalt lose nothing
here.

Aut. I hope so, sir; for I have about me many 260
parcels of charge.

Clo. What hast here? ballads?

Mop. Pray now, buy some: I love a ballad in print
o' life, for then we are sure they are true.

Aut. Here 's one to a very doleful tune, how a
usurer's wife was brought to bed of twenty
money-bags at a burthen, and how she longed
to eat adders' heads and toads carbonadoed.

Mop. Is it true, think you?

Aut. Very true, and but a month old.   270

Dor. Bless me from marrying a usurer!

Aut. Here's the midwife's name to't, one Mistress
Tale-porter, and five or six honest wives that
were present.   Why should I carry lies
abroad?

Mop. Pray you now, buy it.

Clo. Come on, lay it by: and let's first see moe
ballads; we'll buy the other things anon.

Aut. Here's another ballad of a fish, that appeared
upon the coast, on Wednesday the fourscore   280
of April, forty thousand fathom above water,
and sung this ballad against the hard hearts of
maids: it was thought she was a woman, and
was turned into a cold fish for she would not
exchange flesh with one that loved her: the
ballad is very pitiful and as true.

Dor. Is it true too, think you?

Aut. Five justices' hands at it, and witnesses more
than my pack will hold.

Clo. Lay it by too: another.   290

Aut. This is a merry ballad, but a very pretty
one.

Mop. Let's have some merry ones.

Aut. Why, this is a passing merry one and goes
to the tune of 'Two maids wooing a man:'

there's scarce a maid westward but she sings it;
'tis in request, I can tell you.

Mop. We can both sing it: if thou'lt bear a part,
thou shalt hear; 'tis in three parts.

Dor. We had the tune on't a month ago.   300

Aut. I can bear my part; you must know 'tis my
occupation: have at it with you.

SONG.

A. Get you hence, for I must go
Where it fits not you to know.
      D. Whither? *M.* O, whither? *D.* Whither?

M. It becomes thy oath full well,
Thou to me thy secrets tell:
      D. Me too, let me go thither.

M. Or thou goest to the grange or mill:
D. If to either, thou dost ill.   310
      A. Neither. *D.* What, neither? *A.* Neither.

D. Thou hast sworn my love to be;
M. Thou hast sworn it more to me:
Then whither goest? say, whither?

Clo. We'll have this song out anon by ourselves:
my father and the gentlemen are in sad talk,
and we'll not trouble them. Come, bring away

thy pack after me. Wenches, I'll buy for
you both. Pedlar, let's have the first choice. 319
Follow me, girls. [*Exit with Dorcas and Mopsa.*

Aut. And you shall pay well for 'em. [*Follows singing.*

> Will you buy any tape,
>   Or lace for your cape,
> My dainty duck, my dear-a?
>   Any silk, any thread,
>   Any toys for your head,
> Of the new'st, and finest, finest wear-a?
>   Come to the pedlar;
>   Money's a medler,
> That doth utter all men's ware-a. [*Exit.* 330

Re-enter Servant.

Serv. Master, there is three carters, three shepherds,
three neat-herds, three swine-herds, that have
made themselves all men of hair, they call
themselves Saltiers, and they have a dance
which the wenches say is a gallimaufry of
gambols, because they are not in't; but they
themselves are o' the mind, if it be not too
rough for some that know little but bowling,
it will please plentifully.

Shep. Away! we'll none on't: here has been too 340
    much homely foolery already. I know, sir, we
    weary you.

Pol. You weary those that refresh us: pray, let's
    see these four threes of herdsmen.

Serv. One three of them, by their own report, sir,
    hath danced before the king; and not the worst
    of the three but jumps twelve foot and a half by
    the squier.

Shep. Leave your prating: since these good men
    are pleased, let them come in; but quickly 350
    now.

Serv. Why, they stay at door, sir.   [*Exit.*

Here a dance of twelve Satyrs.

Pol. O, father, you'll know more of that hereafter.
    [*To Cam.*] Is it not too far gone? 'Tis time to part
      them.
    He's simple and tells much. How now, fair shep-
      herd!
    Your heart is full of something that does take
    Your mind from feasting. Sooth, when I was young
    And handed love as you do, I was wont
    To load my she with knacks: I would have ran-
      sack'd 360

The pedlar's silken treasury and have pour'd it
To her acceptance; you have let him go
And nothing marted with him.   If your lass
Interpretation should abuse and call this
Your lack of love or bounty, you were straited
For a reply, at least if you make a care
Of happy holding her.

Flo.   Old sir, I know
She prizes not such trifles as these are:
The gifts she looks from me are pack'd and lock'd
Up in my heart; which I have given already,   370
But not deliver'd.   O, hear me breathe my life
Before this ancient sir, who, it should seem,
Hath sometime loved!   I take thy hand, this hand,
As soft as dove's down and as white as it,
Or Ethiopian's tooth, or the fann'd snow that's bolted
By the northern blasts twice o'er.

Pol.   What follows this?
How prettily the young swain seems to wash
The hand was fair before!   I have put you out:
But to your protestation; let me hear
What you profess.

Flo.   Do, and be witness to 't.   380
Pol. And this my neighbour too?
Flo.   And he, and more

96

Than he, and men, the earth, the heavens, and all:
That, were I crown'd the most imperial monarch,
Thereof most worthy, were I the fairest youth
That ever made eye swerve, had force and knowledge
More than was ever man's, I would not prize them
Without her love; for her employ them all;
Commend them and condemn them to her service
Or to their own perdition.

Pol.   Fairly offer'd.

Cam. This shows a sound affection.

Shep.   But, my daughter, 390
Say you the like to him?

Per.   I cannot speak
So well, nothing so well; no, nor mean better:
By the pattern of mine own thoughts I cut out
The purity of his.

Shep.   Take hands, a bargain!
And, friends unknown, you shall bear witness to 't:
I give my daughter to him, and will make
Her portion equal his.

Flo.   O, that must be
I' the virtue of your daughter: one being dead,
I shall have more than you can dream of yet;
Enough then for your wonder.   But, come on, 400
Contract us 'fore these witnesses.

Shep.   Come, your hand;
And, daughter, yours.

Pol.   Soft, swain, awhile, beseech you;
Have you a father?

Flo.   I have: but what of him?

Pol. Knows he of this?

Flo.   He neither does nor shall.

Pol. Methinks a father
Is at the nuptial of his son a guest
That best becomes the table.   Pray you once more,
Is not your father grown incapable
Of reasonable affairs? is he not stupid
With age and altering rheums? can he speak? hear?
Know man from man? dispute his own estate? 411
Lies he not bed-rid? and again does nothing
But what he did being childish?

Flo.   No, good sir;
He has his health and ampler strength indeed
Than most have of his age.

Pol.   By my white beard,
You offer him, if this be so, a wrong
Something unfilial: reason my son
Should choose himself a wife, but as good reason
The father, all whose joy is nothing else
But fair posterity, should hold some counsel   420

98

In such a business.

Flo.　　　　　　　I yield all this;
But for some other reasons, my grave sir,
Which 'tis not fit you know, I not acquaint
My father of this business.

Pol.　　　　　　　　　Let him know 't.

Flo. He shall not.

Pol.　　　　　Prithee, let him.

Flo.　　　　　　　　　No, he must not.

Shep. Let him, my son: he shall not need to grieve
At knowing of thy choice.

Flo.　　　　　　　Come, come, he must not.
Mark our contract.

Pol.　　　　　　Mark your divorce, young sir,
　　　　　　　　　　　[*Discovering himself.*
Whom son I dare not call; thou art too base
To be acknowledged: thou a sceptre's heir,　　430
That thus affects a sheep-hook! Thou old traitor,
I am sorry that by hanging thee I can
But shorten thy life one week. And thou, fresh piece
Of excellent witchcraft, who of force must know
The royal fool thou copest with,—

Shep.　　　　　　　O, my heart!

Pol. I'll have thy beauty scratch'd with briers, and made
More homely than thy state. For thee, fond boy,

If I may ever know thou dost but sigh
That thou no more shalt see this knack, as never
I mean thou shalt, we 'll bar thee from succession;
Not hold thee of our blood, no, not our kin,   441
Far than Deucalion off: mark thou my words:
Follow us to the court.   Thou churl, for this time,
Though full of our displeasure, yet we free thee
From the dead blow of it.   And you, enchantment,—
Worthy enough a herdsman; yea, him too,
That makes himself, but for our honour therein,
Unworthy thee,—if ever henceforth thou
These rural latches to his entrance open,
Or hoop his body more with thy embraces,   450
I will devise a death as cruel for thee
As thou art tender to 't.   [*Exit.*

Per.   Even here undone!
I was not much afeard; for once or twice
I was about to speak and tell him plainly,
The selfsame sun that shines upon his court
Hides not his visage from our cottage, but
Looks on alike.   Will 't please you, sir, be gone?
I told you what would come of this: beseech you,
Of your own state take care: this dream of mine,—
Being now awake, I 'll queen it no inch farther, 460
But milk my ewes and weep.

Cam.   Why, how now, father;
     Speak ere thou diest.

Shep.   I cannot speak, nor think,
     Nor dare to know that which I know. O sir!
     You have undone a man of fourscore three,
     That thought to fill his grave in quiet; yea,
     To die upon the bed my father died,
     To lie close by his honest bones: but now
     Some hangman must put on my shroud and lay me
     Where no priest shovels in dust. O cursed wretch,
     That knew'st this was the prince, and wouldst ad-
           venture   470
     To mingle faith with him! Undone! undone!
     If I might die within this hour, I have lived
     To die when I desire.   [*Exit.*

Flo.   Why look you so upon me?
     I am but sorry, not afeard; delay'd,
     But nothing alter'd: what I was, I am;
     More straining on for plucking back, not following
     My leash unwillingly.

Cam.   Gracious my lord,
     You know your father's temper: at this time
     He will allow no speech, which I do guess
     You do not purpose to him; and as hardly   480
     Will he endure your sight as yet, I fear:

    Then, till the fury of his highness settle,
    Come not before him.

Flo.   I not purpose it.
    I think, Camillo?

Cam.   Even he, my lord.

Per. How often have I told you 'twould be thus!
    How often said, my dignity would last
    But till 'twere known?

Flo.   It cannot fail but by
    The violation of my faith; and then
    Let nature crush the sides o' the earth together
    And mar the seeds within! Lift up thy looks: 490
    From my succession wipe me, father, I
    Am heir to my affection.

Cam.   Be advised.

Flo. I am, and by my fancy: if my reason
    Will thereto be obedient, I have reason;
    If not, my senses, better pleased with madness,
    Do bid it welcome.

Cam.   This is desperate, sir.

Flo. So call it: but it does fulfil my vow;
    I needs must think it honesty. Camillo,
    Not for Bohemia, nor the pomp that may
    Be thereat glean'd; for all the sun sees, or   500
    The close earth wombs, or the profound seas hide

In unknown fathoms, will I break my oath
To this my fair beloved: therefore, I pray you,
As you have ever been my father's honour'd friend,
When he shall miss me,—as, in faith, I mean not
To see him any more,—cast your good counsels
Upon his passion: let myself and fortune
Tug for the time to come. This you may know
And so deliver, I am put to sea
With her whom here I cannot hold on shore;   510
And most opportune to our need I have
A vessel rides fast by, but not prepared
For this design. What course I mean to hold
Shall nothing benefit your knowledge, nor
Concern me the reporting.

Cam.   O my lord!
I would your spirit were easier for advice,
Or stronger for your need.

Flo.   Hark, Perdita. [*Drawing her aside.*
I'll hear you by and by.

Cam.   He's irremoveable,
Resolved for flight. Now were I happy, if
His going I could frame to serve my turn,   520
Save him from danger, do him love and honour,
Purchase the sight again of dear Sicilia
And that unhappy king, my master, whom

I so much thirst to see.

Flo.   Now, good Camillo ;
I am so fraught with curious business that
I leave out ceremony.

Cam.   Sir, I think
You have heard of my poor services, i' the love
That I have borne your father ?

Flo.   Very nobly
Have you deserved : it is my father's music
To speak your deeds, not little of his care   530
To have them recompensed as thought on.

Cam.   Well, my lord,
If you may please to think I love the king,
And through him what is nearest to him, which is
Your gracious self, embrace but my direction,
If your more ponderous and settled project
May suffer alteration, on mine honour
I 'll point you where you shall have such receiving
As shall become your highness ; where you may
Enjoy your mistress, from the whom, I see,
There 's no disjunction to be made, but by   540
As heavens forefend ! your ruin ; marry her,
And, with my best endeavours in your absence,
Your discontenting father strive to qualify
And bring him up to liking.

Flo. How, Camillo,
May this, almost a miracle, be done?
That I may call thee something more than man
And after that trust to thee.

Cam. Have you thought on
A place whereto you 'll go?

Flo. Not any yet:
But as the unthought-on accident is guilty
To what we wildly do, so we profess   550
Ourselves to be the slaves of chance, and flies
Of every wind that blows.

Cam. Then list to me:
This follows, if you will not change your purpose
But undergo this flight, make for Sicilia,
And there present yourself and your fair princess,
For so I see she must be, 'fore Leontes:
She shall be habited as it becomes
The partner of your bed.   Methinks I see
Leontes opening his free arms and weeping   559
His welcomes forth; asks thee the son forgiveness,
As 'twere i' the father's person; kisses the hands
Of your fresh princess; o'er and o'er divides him
'Twixt his unkindness and his kindness; the one
He chides to hell and bids the other grow
Faster than thought or time.

Flo.   Worthy Camillo,
What colour for my visitation shall I
Hold up before him ?

Cam.   Sent by the king your father
To greet him and to give him comforts.   Sir,
The manner of your bearing towards him, with
What you as from your father shall deliver,   570
Things known betwixt us three, I 'll write you down :
The which shall point you forth at every sitting
What you must say ; that he shall not perceive
But that you have your father's bosom there
And speak his very heart.

Flo.   I am bound to you :
There is some sap in this.

Cam.   A course more promising
Than a wild dedication of yourselves
To unpath'd waters, undream'd shores, most certain
To miseries enough : no hope to help you,
But as you shake off one to take another :   580
Nothing so certain as your anchors, who
Do their best office, if they can but stay you
Where you 'll be loath to be : besides you know
Prosperity 's the very bond of love,
Whose fresh complexion and whose heart together
Affliction alters.

Per. One of these is true:
I think affliction may subdue the cheek,
But not take in the mind.

Cam. Yea, say you so?
There shall not at your father's house these seven years
Be born another such.

Flo. My good Camillo,   590
She is as forward of her breeding as
She is i' the rear o' her birth.

Cam. I cannot say 'tis pity
She lacks instructions, for she seems a mistress
To most that teach.

Per. Your pardon, sir; for this
I 'll blush you thanks.

Flo. My prettiest Perdita!
But O, the thorns we stand upon! Camillo,
Preserver of my father, now of me,
The medicine of our house, how shall we do?
We are not furnish'd like Bohemia's son,
Nor shall appear in Sicilia.

Cam. My lord,   600
Fear none of this: I think you know my fortunes
Do all lie there: it shall be so my care
To have you royally appointed as if
The scene you play were mine. For instance, sir,

That you may know you shall not want, one word.

[*They talk aside.*

Re-enter Autolycus.

Aut. Ha, ha! what a fool Honesty is! and Trust,
his sworn brother, a very simple gentleman! I
have sold all my trumpery; not a counterfeit
stone, not a ribbon, glass, pomander, brooch,
table-book, ballad, knife, tape, glove, shoe-tie, 610
bracelet, horn-ring, to keep my pack from
fasting: they throng who should buy first, as
if my trinkets had been hallowed and brought
a benediction to the buyer: by which means I
saw whose purse was best in picture; and what I
saw, to my good use I remembered. My clown,
who wants but something to be a reasonable man,
grew so in love with the wenches' song, that he
would not stir his pettitoes till he had both tune
and words; which so drew the rest of the herd 620
to me, that all their other senses stuck in ears:
you might have pinched a placket, it was sense-
less; 'twas nothing to geld a codpiece of a purse;
I would have filed keys off that hung in chains:
no hearing, no feeling, but my sir's song, and
admiring the nothing of it. So that in this
time of lethargy I picked and cut most of their

festival purses; and had not the old man come in
with a whoo-bub against his daughter and the
king's son and scared my choughs from the chaff, 630
I had not left a purse alive in the whole army.

      [*Camillo, Florizel, and Perdita come forward.*

Cam. Nay, but my letters, by this means being there
So soon as you arrive, shall clear that doubt.

Flo. And those that you 'll procure from King Leontes—

Cam. Shall satisfy your father.

Per.   Happy be you!
All that you speak shows fair.

Cam.   Who have we here?

                           [*Seeing Autolycus.*

We 'll make an instrument of this; omit
Nothing may give us aid.

Aut. If they have overheard me now, why,
hanging.   640

Cam. How now, good fellow! why shakest thou
so? Fear not, man; here 's no harm intended
to thee.

Aut. I am a poor fellow, sir.

Cam. Why, be so still; here 's nobody will steal
that from thee: yet for the outside of thy
poverty we must make an exchange; therefore
discase thee instantly,—thou must think there 's

a necessity in 't,—and change garments with this
gentleman : though the pennyworth on his side   650
be the worst, yet hold thee, there 's some boot.

Aut. I am a poor fellow, sir.   [*Aside*] I know ye
well enough.

Cam. Nay, prithee, dispatch : the gentleman is half
flayed already.

Aut. Are you in earnest, sir ?   [*Aside*] I smell
the trick on 't.

Flo. Dispatch, I prithee.

Aut. Indeed, I have had earnest ; but I cannot with
conscience take it.   660

Cam. Unbuckle, unbuckle.

        [*Florizel and Autolycus exchange garments.*

Fortunate mistress,—let my prophecy
Come home to ye !—you must retire yourself
Into some covert : take your sweetheart's hat
And pluck it o'er your brows, muffle your face,
Dismantle you, and, as you can, disliken
The truth of your own seeming ; that you may—
For I do fear eyes over—to shipboard
Get undescried.

Per.   I see the play so lies
That I must bear a part.

Cam.   No remedy.   670

Have you done there?

Flo.   Should I now meet my father,
He would not call me son.

Cam.   Nay, you shall have no hat.
                  [*Giving it to Perdita.*
Come, lady, come.   Farewell, my friend.

Aut.   Adieu, sir.

Flo. O Perdita, what have we twain forgot!
Pray you, a word.

Cam. [*Aside*] What I do next, shall be to tell the king
Of this escape and whither they are bound;
Wherein my hope is I shall so prevail
To force him after: in whose company
I shall review Sicilia, for whose sight   680
I have a woman's longing.

Flo.   Fortune speed us!
Thus we set on, Camillo, to the sea-side.

Cam. The swifter speed the better.
               [*Exeunt Florizel, Perdita, and Camillo.*

Aut. I understand the business, I hear it: to have
an open ear, a quick eye, and a nimble hand, is
necessary for a cut-purse; a good nose is re-
quisite also, to smell out work for the other
senses. I see this is the time that the unjust
man doth thrive. What an exchange had this

been without boot! What a boot is here with 690
this exchange! Sure the gods do this year
connive at us, and we may do any thing extem-
pore. The prince himself is about a piece of
iniquity, stealing away from his father with his
clog at his heels: if I thought it were a piece
of honesty to acquaint the king withal, I would
not do 't: I hold it the more knavery to con-
ceal it; and therein am I constant to my pro-
fession.

Re-enter Clown and Shepherd.

Aside, aside; here is more matter for a hot
brain: every lane's end, every shop, church, 700
session, hanging, yields a careful man work.

Clo. See, see; what a man you are now! There
is no other way but to tell the king she's
a changeling and none of your flesh and
blood.

Shep. Nay, but hear me.

Clo. Nay, but hear me.

Shep. Go to, then.

Clo. She being none of your flesh and blood, your 710
flesh and blood has not offended the king; and
so your flesh and blood is not to be punished by

him.   Show those things you found about her,
those secret things, all but what she has with
her : this being done, let the law go whistle : I
warrant you.

Shep. I will tell the king all, every word, yea, and
his son's pranks too ; who, I may say, is no
honest man, neither to his father nor to me, to
go about to make me the king's brother-in-   720
law.

Clo. Indeed, brother-in-law was the farthest off you
could have been to him and then your blood
had been the dearer by I know how much an
ounce.

Aut. [*Aside*] Very wisely, puppies !

Shep. Well, let us to the king : there is that in this
fardel will make him scratch his beard.

Aut. [*Aside*] I know not what impediment this
complaint may be to the flight of my master.   730

Clo. Pray heartily he be at palace.

Aut. [*Aside*] Though I am not naturally honest,
I am so sometimes by chance : let me pocket
up my pedlar's excrement. [*Takes off his
false beard.*] How now, rustics ! whither are
you bound ?

Shep. To the palace, an it like your worship.

Aut. Your affairs there, what, with whom, the
condition of that fardel, the place of your
dwelling, your names, your ages, of what 740
having, breeding, and any thing that is fitting
to be known, discover.

Clo. We are but plain fellows, sir.

Aut. A lie; you are rough and hairy. Let me
have no lying: it becomes none but tradesmen,
and they often give us soldiers the lie: but
we pay them for it with stamped coin, not stab-
bing steel; therefore they do not give us the
lie.

Clo. Your worship had like to have given us one, 750
if you had not taken yourself with the
manner.

Shep. Are you a courtier, an't like you, sir?

Aut. Whether it like me or no, I am a courtier.
Seest thou not the air of the court in these
enfoldings? hath not my gait in it the measure
of the court? receives not thy nose court-
odour from me? reflect I not on thy baseness
court-contempt? Thinkest thou, for that I insinuate, or toaze from thee thy business, I am 760
therefore no courtier? I am courtier cap-a-pe;
and one that will either push on or pluck back

thy business there: whereupon I command thee
to open thy affair.

Shep. My business, sir, is to the king.

Aut. What advocate hast thou to him?

Shep. I know not, an't like you.

Clo. Advocate's the court-word for a pheasant:
say you have none.

Shep. None, sir; I have no pheasant, cock nor 770
hen.

Aut. How blessed are we that are not simple men!
Yet nature might have made me as these are,
Therefore I will not disdain.

Clo. This cannot be but a great courtier.

Shep. His garments are rich, but he wears them not
handsomely.

Clo. He seems to be the more noble in being fan-
tastical: a great man, I'll warrant; I know
by the picking on's teeth.   780

Aut. The fardel there? what's i' the fardel?
Wherefore that box?

Shep. Sir, there lies such secrets in this fardel and
box, which none must know but the king;
and which he shall know within this hour, if
I may come to the speech of him.

Aut. Age, thou hast lost thy labour.

Shep. Why, sir?

Aut. The king is not at the palace; he is gone
aboard a new ship to purge melancholy and air 790
himself: for, if thou beest capable of things
serious, thou must know the king is full of grief.

Shep. So 'tis said, sir; about his son, that should
have married a shepherd's daughter.

Aut. If that shepherd be not in hand-fast, let him
fly: the curses he shall have, the tortures he
shall feel, will break the back of man, the heart
of monster.

Clo. Think you so, sir?

Aut. Not he alone shall suffer what wit can make 800
heavy and vengeance bitter; but those that are
germane to him, though removed fifty times,
shall all come under the hangman: which though
it be great pity, yet it is necessary. An old
sheep-whistling rogue, a ram-tender, to offer to
have his daughter come into grace! Some say
he shall be stoned; but that death is too soft for
him, say I: draw our throne into a sheep-cote!
all deaths are too few, the sharpest too easy.

Clo. Has the old man e'er a son, sir, do you hear, 810
an 't like you, sir?

Aut. He has a son, who shall be flayed alive; then,

'nointed over with honey, set on the head of a wasp's nest; then stand till he be three quarters and a dram dead; then recovered again with aqua-vitæ or some other hot infusion; then, raw as he is, and in the hottest day prognostication proclaims, shall he be set against a brick-wall, the sun looking with a southward eye upon him, where he is to behold him with flies blown 820 to death. But what talk we of these traitorly rascals, whose miseries are to be smiled at, their offences being so capital? Tell me, for you seem to be honest plain men, what you have to the king: being something gently considered, I'll bring you where he is aboard, tender your persons to his presence, whisper him in your behalfs; and if it be in man besides the king to effect your suits, here is man shall do it.

Clo. He seems to be of great authority: close with 830 him, give him gold; and though authority be a stubborn bear, yet he is oft led by the nose with gold: show the inside of your purse to the outside of his hand, and no more ado. Remember 'stoned,' and 'flayed alive.'

Shep. An't please you, sir, to undertake the business for us, here is that gold I have: I'll make it

as much more and leave this young man in pawn
till I bring it you.

Aut. After I have done what I promised?　840

Shep. Ay, sir.

Aut. Well, give me the moiety. Are you a party
in this business?

Clo. In some sort, sir: but though my case be a
pitiful one, I hope I shall not be flayed out of it.

Aut. O, that's the case of the shepherd's son: hang
him, he'll be made an example.

Clo. Comfort, good comfort! We must to the king
and show our strange sights: he must know 'tis
none of your daughter nor my sister; we are　850
gone else. Sir, I will give you as much as this
old man does when the business is performed,
and remain, as he says, your pawn till it be
brought you.

Aut. I will trust you. Walk before toward the
sea-side; go on the right hand: I will but look
upon the hedge and follow you.

Clo. We are blest in this man, as I may say, even
blest.

Shep. Let's before as he bids us: he was provided　860
to do us good.　[*Exeunt Shepherd and Clown.*

Aut. If I had a mind to be honest, I see Fortune

would not suffer me: she drops booties in my
mouth.   I am courted now with a double occasion, gold and a means to do the prince my
master good; which who knows how that may
turn back to my advancement?   I will bring
these two moles, these blind ones, aboard him:
if he think it fit to shore them again and that
the complaint they have to the king concerns 870
him nothing, let him call me rogue for being so
far officious; for I am proof against that title
and what shame else belongs to 't.   To him will
I present them: there may be matter in it. [*Exit.*

Act Fifth.

Scene I.

A room in Leontes' palace.

Enter Leontes, Cleomenes, Dion, Paulina, and Servants.

Cleo. Sir, you have done enough, and have perform'd
A saint-like sorrow: no fault could you make,
Which you have not redeem'd; indeed, paid down
More penitence than done trespass: at the last,
Do as the heavens have done, forget your evil;

With them forgive yourself.

Leon.   Whilst I remember
Her and her virtues, I cannot forget
My blemishes in them, and so still think of
The wrong I did myself: which was so much,
That heirless it hath made my kingdom; and   10
Destroy'd the sweet'st companion that e'er man
Bred his hopes out of.

Paul.   True, too true, my lord:
If, one by one, you wedded all the world,
Or from the all that are took something good,
To make a perfect woman, she you kill'd
Would be unparallel'd.

Leon.   I think so. Kill'd!
She I kill'd! I did so: but thou strikest me
Sorely, to say I did; it is as bitter
Upon thy tongue as in my thought: now, good now,
Say so but seldom.

Cleo.   Not at all, good lady: 20
You might have spoken a thousand things that would
Have done the time more benefit and graced
Your kindness better.

Paul.   You are one of those
Would have him wed again.

Dion.   If you would not so,

You pity not the state, nor the remembrance
Of his most sovereign name; consider little
What dangers, by his highness' fail of issue,
May drop upon his kingdom and devour
Incertain lookers on.　What were more holy
Than to rejoice the former queen is well?　　　30
What holier than, for royalty's repair,
For present comfort and for future good,
To bless the bed of majesty again
With a sweet fellow to 't?

Paul.　　　　　　　　　There is none worthy,
Respecting her that's gone.　Besides, the gods
Will have fulfill'd their secret purposes;
For has not the divine Apollo said,
Is 't not the terror of his oracle,
That King Leontes shall not have an heir
Till his lost child be found? which that it shall,　40
Is all as monstrous to our human reason
As my Antigonus to break his grave
And come again to me; who, on my life,
Did perish with the infant.　'Tis your counsel
My lord should to the heavens be contrary,
Oppose against their wills. [*To Leontes*] Care not
　　for issue;
The crown will find an heir: great Alexander

Left his to the worthiest; so his successor
Was like to be the best.

Leon.　　　　　　　　Good Paulina,
Who hast the memory of Hermione,　　　　　　50
I know, in honour, O, that ever I
Had squared me to thy counsel!—then, even now,
I might have look'd upon my queen's full eyes;
Have taken treasure from her lips,—

Paul.　　　　　　　　　　And left them
More rich for what they yielded.

Leon.　　　　　　　　　Thou speak'st truth.
No more such wives; therefore, no wife: one worse,
And better used, would make her sainted spirit
Again possess her corpse, and on this stage,
Where we offenders now, appear soul-vex'd,
And begin, 'Why to me?'

Paul.　　　　　　　Had she such power,　60
She had just cause.

Leon.　　　　　　She had; and would incense me
To murder her I married.

Paul.　　　　　　I should so.
Were I the ghost that walk'd, I'ld bid you mark
Her eye, and tell me for what dull part in 't
You chose her; then I'ld shriek, that even your ears
Should rift to hear me; and the words that follow'd

122

Should be 'Remember mine.'

Leon.   Stars, stars,
And all eyes else dead coals! Fear thou no wife;
I 'll have no wife, Paulina.

Paul.   Will you swear
Never to marry but by my free leave?   70

Leon. Never, Paulina; so be blest my spirit!

Paul. Then, good my lords, bear witness to his oath.

Cleo. You tempt him over-much.

Paul.   Unless another,
As like Hermione as is her picture,
Affront his eye.

Cleo.   Good madam,—

Paul.   I have done.
Yet, if my lord will marry,—if you will, sir,
No remedy, but you will,—give me the office
To choose you a queen: she shall not be so young
As was your former; but she shall be such
As, walk'd your first queen's ghost, it should take joy
To see her in your arms.

Leon.   My true Paulina,   81
We shall not marry till thou bid'st us.

Paul.   That
Shall be when your first queen 's again in breath;
Never till then.

Enter a Gentleman.

Gent. One that gives out himself Prince Florizel,
　　Son of Polixenes, with his princess, she
　　The fairest I have yet beheld, desires access
　　To your high presence.

Leon.　　　　　　What with him? he comes not
　　Like to his father's greatness: his approach,
　　So out of circumstance and sudden, tells us　　90
　　'Tis not a visitation framed, but forced
　　By need and accident.　What train?

Gent.　　　　　　　　　　But few,
　　And those but mean.

Leon.　　　　　His princess, say you, with him?

Gent. Ay, the most peerless piece of earth, I think,
　　That e'er the sun shone bright on.

Paul.　　　　　　　　O Hermione,
　　As every present time doth boast itself
　　Above a better gone, so must thy grave
　　Give way to what's seen now!　Sir, you yourself
　　Have said and writ so, but your writing now
　　Is colder than that theme, 'She had not been,　100
　　Nor was not to be equall'd;'—thus your verse
　　Flow'd with her beauty once: 'tis shrewdly ebb'd,
　　To say you have seen a better.

Gent.   Pardon, madam:
The one I have almost forgot,—your pardon,—
The other, when she has obtain'd your eye,
Will have your tongue too.   This is a creature,
Would she begin a sect, might quench the zeal
Of all professors else ; make proselytes
Of who she but bid follow.

Paul.   How ! not women ?

Gent. Women will love her, that she is a woman   110
More worth than any man ; men, that she is
The rarest of all women.

Leon.   Go, Cleomenes ;
Yourself, assisted with your honour'd friends,
Bring them to our embracement.

           [*Exeunt Cleomenes and others.*
                Still, 'tis strange
He thus should steal upon us.

Paul.   Had our prince,
Jewel of children, seen this hour, he had pair'd
Well with this lord : there was not full a·month
Between their births.

Leon. Prithee, no more ; cease ; thou know'st
He dies to me again when talk'd of : sure,   120
When I shall see this gentleman, thy speeches
Will bring me to consider that which may

Unfurnish me of reason.   They are come.

Re-enter Cleomenes and others, with Florizel
and Perdita.

Your mother was most true to wedlock, prince;
For she did print your royal father off,
Conceiving you : were I but twenty one,
Your father's image is so hit in you,
His very air, that I should call you brother,
As I did him, and speak of something wildly
By us perform'd before.   Most dearly welcome! 130
And your fair princess,—goddess !—O, alas !
I lost a couple, that 'twixt heaven and earth
Might thus have stood begetting wonder, as
You, gracious couple, do : and then I lost,
All mine own folly, the society,
Amity too, of your brave father, whom,
Though bearing misery, I desire my life
Once more to look on him.

Flo.   By his command
Have I here touch'd Sicilia, and from him
Give you all greetings, that a king, at friend,   140
Can send his brother : and, but infirmity,
Which waits upon worn times, hath something seized
His wish'd ability, he had himself

    The lands and waters 'twixt your throne and his
    Measured to look upon you; whom he loves,
    He bade me say so, more than all the sceptres
    And those that bear them living.

Leon.   O my brother,
    Good gentleman! the wrongs I have done thee stir
    Afresh within me; and these thy offices,
    So rarely kind, are as interpreters   150
    Of my behind-hand slackness! Welcome hither,
    As is the spring to the earth. And hath he too
    Exposed this paragon to the fearful usage,
    At least ungentle, of the dreadful Neptune,
    To greet a man not worth her pains, much less
    The adventure of her person?

Flo.   Good my lord,
    She came from Libya.

Leon.   Where the warlike Smalus,
    That noble honour'd lord, is fear'd and loved?

Flo. Most royal sir, from thence; from him, whose
            daughter   159
    His tears proclaim'd his, parting with her: thence,
    A prosperous south-wind friendly, we have cross'd,
    To execute the charge my father gave me,
    For visiting your highness: my best train
    I have from your Sicilian shores dismiss'd;

Who for Bohemia bend, to signify
Not only my success in Libya, sir,
But my arrival, and my wife's, in safety
Here where we are.

Leon.   The blessed gods
Purge all infection from our air whilst you
Do climate here ! You have a holy father,   170
A graceful gentleman ; against whose person,
So sacred as it is, I have done sin :
For which the heavens, taking angry note,
Have left me issueless ; and your father 's blest,
As he from heaven merits it, with you
Worthy his goodness. What might I have been,
Might I a son and daughter now have look'd on,
Such goodly things as you !

Enter a Lord.

Lord.   Most noble sir,
That which I shall report will bear no credit,
Were not the proof so nigh. Please you, great sir,
Bohemia greets you from himself by me ;   181
Desires you to attach his son, who has——
His dignity and duty both cast off——
Fled from his father, from his hopes, and with
A shepherd's daughter.

Leon.   Where's Bohemia? speak.

Lord. Here in your city; I now came from him:
    I speak amazedly; and it becomes
    My marvel and my message. To your court
    Whiles he was hastening, in the chase, it seems,
    Of this fair couple, meets he on the way   190
    The father of this seeming lady and
    Her brother, having both their country quitted
    With this young prince.

Flo.   Camillo has betray'd me;
    Whose honour and whose honesty till now
    Endured all weathers.

Lord.   Lay't so to his charge:
    He's with the king your father.

Leon.   Who? Camillo?

Lord. Camillo, sir; I spake with him; who now
    Has these poor men in question. Never saw I
    Wretches so quake: they kneel, they kiss the earth;
    Forswear themselves as often as they speak: 200
    Bohemia stops his ears, and threatens them
    With divers deaths in death.

Per.   O my poor father!
    The heaven sets spies upon us, will not have
    Our contract celebrated.

Leon.   You are married?

Flo. We are not, sir, nor are we like to be;
    The stars, I see, will kiss the valleys first:
    The odds for high and low 's alike.

Leon.   My lord,
    Is this the daughter of a king?

Flo.   She is,
    When once she is my wife.

Leon. That 'once,' I see by your good father's speed, 210
    Will come on very slowly. I am sorry,
    Most sorry, you have broken from his liking
    Where you were tied in duty, and as sorry
    Your choice is not so rich in worth as beauty,
    That you might well enjoy her.

Flo.   Dear, look up:
    Though Fortune, visible an enemy,
    Should chase us with my father, power no jot
    Hath she to change our loves. Beseech you, sir,
    Remember since you owed no more to time
    Than I do now: with thought of such affections, 220
    Step forth mine advocate; at your request
    My father will grant precious things as trifles.

Leon. Would he do so, I 'ld beg your precious mistress,
    Which he counts but a trifle.

Paul.   Sir, my liege,
    Your eye hath too much youth in 't; not a month

'Fore your queen died, she was more worth such
     gazes
Than what you look on now.

Leon.   I thought of her,
     Even in these looks I made. *[To Florizel]* But
         your petition
     Is yet unanswer'd. I will to your father :
     Your honour not o'erthrown by your desires,   230
     I am friend to them and you : upon which errand
     I now go toward him ; therefore follow me
     And mark what way I make : come, good my lord.
                              [Exeunt.

Scene II.

Before Leontes' palace.

Enter Autolycus and a Gentleman.

Aut. Beseech you, sir, were you present at this
     relation ?

First Gent. I was by at the opening of the fardel,
     heard the old shepherd deliver the manner how
     he found it : whereupon, after a little amazed-
     ness, we were all commanded out of the chamber ;
     only this methought I heard the shepherd say,
     he found the child.

Aut. I would most gladly know the issue of it.

First Gent. I make a broken delivery of the business ;   10
but the changes I perceived in the king and
Camillo were very notes of admiration : they
seemed almost, with staring on one another, to
tear the cases of their eyes ; there was speech in
their dumbness, language in their very gesture ;
they looked as they had heard of a world ran-
somed, or one destroyed : a notable passion of
wonder appeared in them ; but the wisest be-
holder, that knew no more but seeing, could not
say if the importance were joy or sorrow ; but   20
in the extremity of the one, it must needs be.

Enter another Gentleman.

Here comes a gentleman that haply knows more.
The news, Rogero ?

Sec. Gent. Nothing but bonfires : the oracle is fulfilled ; the king's daughter is found : such a deal
of wonder is broken out within this hour, that
ballad-makers cannot be able to express it.

Enter a third Gentleman.

Here comes the Lady Paulina's steward : he can
deliver you more.   How goes it now, sir ? this

news which is called true is so like an old tale,   30
that the verity of it is in strong suspicion : has
the king found his heir ?

Third Gent. Most true, if ever truth were pregnant
by circumstance : that which you hear you 'll
swear you see, there is such unity in the proofs.
The mantle of Queen Hermione's, her jewel
about the neck of it, the letters of Antigonus
found with it, which they know to be his character, the majesty of the creature in resemblance
of the mother, the affection of nobleness which   40
nature shows above her breeding, and many
other evidences proclaim her with all certainty
to be the king's daughter. Did you see the
meeting of the two kings ?

Sec. Gent. No.

Third Gent. Then have you lost a sight, which was
to be seen, cannot be spoken of. There might
you have beheld one joy crown another, so and
in such manner, that it seemed sorrow wept to
take leave of them, for their joy waded in tears.   50
There was casting up of eyes, holding up of
hands, with countenance of such distraction, that
they were to be known by garment, not by favour.
Our king, being ready to leap out of himself for

joy of his found daughter, as if that joy were now
become a loss, cries 'O, thy mother, thy mother!'
then asks Bohemia forgiveness; then embraces
his son-in-law; then again worries he his daughter
with clipping her; now he thanks the old
shepherd, which stands by like a weather-bitten   60
conduit of many kings' reigns.   I never heard
of such another encounter, which lames report
to follow it and undoes description to do it.

Sec. Gent. What, pray you, became of Antigonus,
that carried hence the child?

Third Gent. Like an old tale still, which will have
matter to rehearse, though credit be asleep and
not an ear open.   He was torn to pieces with
a bear: this avouches the shepherd's son; who
has not only his innocence, which seems much,   70
to justify him, but a handkerchief and rings of
his that Paulina knows.

First Gent. What became of his bark and his
followers?

Third Gent. Wrecked the same instant of their
master's death and in the view of the shepherd:
so that all the instruments which aided to ex-
pose the child were even then lost when it was
found.   But O, the noble combat that 'twixt

joy and sorrow was fought in Paulina! She had 80
one eye declined for the loss of her husband,
another elevated that the oracle was fulfilled: she
lifted the princess from the earth, and so locks her
in embracing, as if she would pin her to her heart
that she might no more be in danger of losing.

First Gent. The dignity of this act was worth the
audience of kings and princes; for by such was
it acted.

Third Gent. One of the prettiest touches of all and
that which angled for mine eyes, caught the 90
water though not the fish, was when, at the relation of the queen's death, with the manner how
she came to 't bravely confessed and lamented
by the king, how attentiveness wounded his
daughter; till, from one sign of dolour to another,
she did, with an 'Alas,' I would fain say, bleed
tears, for I am sure my heart wept blood. Who
was most marble there changed colour; some
swooned, all sorrowed: if all the world could
have seen 't, the woe had been universal. 100

First Gent. Are they returned to the court?

Third Gent. No: the princess hearing of her mother's
statue, which is in the keeping of Paulina,—
a piece many years in doing and now newly

performed by that rare Italian master, Julio
Romano, who, had he himself eternity and
could put breath into his work, would beguile
Nature of her custom, so perfectly he is her ape:
he so near to Hermione hath done Hermione,
that they say one would speak to her and stand　110
in hope of answer:—thither with all greediness of
affection are they gone, and there they intend to sup.

Sec. Gent. I thought she had some great matter there
in hand; for she hath privately twice or thrice
a day, ever since the death of Hermione, visited
that removed house. Shall we thither and with
our company piece the rejoicing?

First Gent. Who would be thence that has the benefit of access? every wink of an eye, some new grace
will be born: our absence makes us unthrifty to　120
our knowledge. Let's along. [*Exeunt Gentlemen.*

Aut. Now, had I not the dash of my former life
in me, would preferment drop on my head. I
brought the old man and his son aboard the
prince; told him I heard them talk of a fardel
and I know not what: but he at that time over-
fond of the shepherd's daughter, so he then took
her to be, who began to be much sea-sick, and
himself little better, extremity of weather con-

tinuing, this mystery remained undiscovered. 130
But 'tis all one to me; for had I been the finder
out of this secret, it would not have relished
among my other discredits.

Enter Shepherd and Clown.

Here comes those I have done good to against
my will, and already appearing in the blossoms
of their fortune.

Shep. Come, boy; I am past moe children, but thy
sons and daughters will be all gentlemen born.

Clo. You are well met, sir. You denied to fight with
me this other day, because I was no gentleman 140
born. See you these clothes? say you see them
not and think me still no gentleman born: you
were best say these robes are not gentleman
born: give me the lie, do, and try whether I
am not now a gentleman born.

Aut. I know you are now, sir, a gentleman born.

Clo. Ay, and have been so any time these four
hours.

Shep. And so have I, boy.

Clo. So you have: but I was a gentleman born before 150
my father; for the king's son took me by the
hand, and called me brother; and then the two

kings called my father brother; and then the prince
my brother and the princess my sister called my
father father ; and so we wept, and there was the
first gentleman-like tears that ever we shed.

Shep. We may live, son, to shed many more.

Clo. Ay ; or else 'twere hard luck, being in so preposterous estate as we are.

Aut. I humbly beseech you, sir, to pardon me all   160
the faults I have committed to your worship,
and to give me your good report to the prince
my master.

Shep. Prithee, son, do ; for we must be gentle, now
we are gentlemen.

Clo. Thou wilt amend thy life ?

Aut. Ay, an it like your good worship.

Clo. Give me thy hand : I will swear to the prince
thou art as honest a true fellow as any is in
Bohemia.   170

Shep. You may say it, but not swear it.

Clo. Not swear it, now I am a gentleman ? Let
boors and franklins say it, I 'll swear it.

Shep. How if it be false, son ?

Clo. If it be ne'er so false, a true gentleman may
swear it in the behalf of his friend : and I 'll
swear to the prince thou art a tall fellow of thy

hands and that thou wilt not be drunk; but I
know thou art no tall fellow of thy hands and
that thou wilt be drunk: but I'll swear it, and I   180
would thou wouldst be a tall fellow of thy hands.

Aut. I will prove so, sir, to my power.

Clo. Ay, by any means prove a tall fellow: if I
do not wonder how thou darest venture to be
drunk, not being a tall fellow, trust me not.
Hark! the kings and the princes, our kindred,
are going to see the queen's picture. Come,
follow us: we'll be thy good masters.   [*Exeunt.*

Scene III.

A chapel in Paulina's house.

*Enter Leontes, Polixenes, Florizel, Perdita, Camillo,
Paulina, Lords, and Attendants.*

Leon. O grave and good Paulina, the great comfort
　　That I have had of thee!

Paul.　　　　　　　　　What, sovereign sir,
　　I did not well, I meant well.   All my services
　　You have paid home: but that you have vouchsafed
　　With your crown'd brother and these your contracted

Heirs of your kingdoms, my poor house to visit,
It is a surplus of your grace, which never
My life may last to answer.

Leon.　　　　　　　　　　O Paulina,
We honour you with trouble : but we came
To see the statue of our queen : your gallery　　10
Have we pass'd through, not without much content
In many singularities ; but we saw not
That which my daughter came to look upon,
The statue of her mother.

Paul.　　　　　　　　　As she lived peerless,
So her dead likeness, I do well believe,
Excels whatever yet you look'd upon
Or hand of man hath done ; therefore I keep it
Lonely, apart.　　But here it is : prepare
To see the life as lively mock'd as ever
Still sleep mock'd death : behold, and say 'tis well.

　　　　　　[*Paulina draws a curtain, and discovers*
　　　　　　　　Hermione standing like a statue.

I like your silence, it the more shows off　　21
Your wonder : but yet speak ; first, you, my liege.
Comes it not something near ?

Leon.　　　　　　　　　Her natural posture !
Chide me, dear stone, that I may say indeed
Thou art Hermione ; or rather, thou art she

In thy not chiding, for she was as tender
As infancy and grace.   But yet, Paulina,
Hermione was not so much wrinkled, nothing
So aged as this seems.

Pol.   O, not by much.

Paul. So much the more our carver's excellence;   30
Which lets go by some sixteen years and makes her
As she lived now.

Leon.   As now she might have done,
So much to my good comfort, as it is
Now piercing to my soul.   O, thus she stood,
Even with such life of majesty, warm life,
As now it coldly stands, when first I woo'd her!
I am ashamed: does not the stone rebuke me
For being more stone than it?   O royal piece,
There's magic in thy majesty, which has
My evils conjured to remembrance, and   40
From thy admiring daughter took the spirits,
Standing like stone with thee.

Per.   And give me leave,
And do not say 'tis superstition, that
I kneel and then implore her blessing.   Lady,
Dear queen, that ended when I but began,
Give me that hand of yours to kiss.

Paul.   O, patience!

141

The statue is but newly fix'd, the colour 's
Not dry.

Cam. My lord, your sorrow was too sore laid on,
Which sixteen winters cannot blow away,   50
So many summers dry: scarce any joy
Did ever so long live; no sorrow
But kill'd itself much sooner.

Pol.   Dear my brother,
Let him that was the cause of this have power
To take off so much grief from you as he
Will piece up in himself.

Paul.   Indeed, my lord,
If I had thought the sight of my poor image
Would thus have wrought you, for the stone is **mine**,
I 'ld not have show'd it.

Leon.   Do not draw the curtain.

Paul. No longer shall you gaze on 't, lest your fancy 60
May think anon it moves.

Leon.   Let be, let be.
Would I were dead, but that, methinks, already—
What was he that did make it? See, my lord,
Would you not deem it breathed? and that those **veins**
Did verily bear blood?

Pol.   Masterly done:
The very life seems warm upon her lip.

Leon. The fixure of her eye has motion in't,
　As we are mock'd with art.

Paul.　　　　　　　I'll draw the curtain:
　My lord's almost so far transported that
　He'll think anon it lives.

Leon.　　　　　O sweet Paulina,　　70
　Make me to think so twenty years together!
　No settled senses of the world can match
　The pleasure of that madness. Let't alone.

Paul. I am sorry, sir, I have thus far stirr'd you: but
　I could afflict you farther.

Leon.　　　　　Do, Paulina;
　For this affliction has a taste as sweet
　As any cordial comfort. Still, methinks,
　There is an air comes from her: what fine chisel
　Could ever yet cut breath? Let no man mock me,
　For I will kiss her.

Paul.　　　　Good my lord, forbear:　　80
　The ruddiness upon her lip is wet;
　You'll mar it if you kiss it, stain your own
　With oily painting. Shall I draw the curtain?

Leon. No, not these twenty years.

Per.　　　　　So long could I
　Stand by, a looker on.

Paul.　　　　Either forbear,

143

Quit presently the chapel, or resolve you
For more amazement. If you can behold it,
I 'll make the statue move indeed, descend
And take you by the hand : but then you 'll think,
Which I protest against, I am assisted   90
By wicked powers.

Leon.   What you can make her do,
I am content to look on : what to speak,
I am content to hear ; for 'tis as easy
To make her speak as move.

Paul.   It is required
You do awake your faith. Then all stand still ;
On : those that think it is unlawful business
I am about, let them depart.

Leon.   Proceed :
No foot shall stir.

Paul.   Music, awake her ; strike ! [*Music.*
'Tis time ; descend ; be stone no more ; approach ;
Strike all that look upon with marvel. Come,   100
I 'll fill your grave up : stir, nay, come away,
Bequeath to death your numbness, for from him
Dear life redeems you. You perceive she stirs :

                              [*Hermione comes down.*

Start not ; her actions shall be holy as
You hear my spell is lawful : do not shun her

Until you see her die again; for then
You kill her double. Nay, present your hand:
When she was young you woo'd her; now in age
Is she become the suitor?

Leon.   O, she's warm!
If this be magic, let it be an art   110
Lawful as eating.

Pol.   She embraces him.

Cam. She hangs about his neck:
If she pertain to life let her speak too.

Pol. Ay, and make 't manifest where she has lived,
Or how stolen from the dead.

Paul.   That she is living,
Were it but told you, should be hooted at
Like an old tale: but it appears she lives,
Though yet she speak not. Mark a little while.
Please you to interpose, fair madam: kneel
And pray your mother's blessing. Turn, good lady;
Our Perdita is found.

Her.   You gods, look down,   121
And from your sacred vials pour your graces
Upon my daughter's head! Tell me, mine own,
Where hast thou been preserved? where lived? how
     found
Thy father's court? for thou shalt hear that I,

Knowing by Paulina that the oracle
Gave hope thou wast in being, have preserved
Myself to see the issue.

Paul.   There's time enough for that;
Lest they desire upon this push to trouble
Your joys with like relation.   Go together,   130
You precious winners all; your exultation
Partake to every one.   I, an old turtle,
Will wing me to some wither'd bough and there
My mate, that's never to be found again,
Lament till I am lost.

Leon.   O, peace, Paulina!
Thou shouldst a husband take by my consent,
As I by thine a wife: this is a match,
And made between's by vows.   Thou hast found
      mine;
But how, is to be question'd; for I saw her,
As I thought, dead; and have in vain said many 140
A prayer upon her grave.   I'll not seek far,—
For him, I partly know his mind,—to find thee
An honourable husband.   Come, Camillo,
And take her by the hand, whose worth and honesty
Is richly noted and here justified
By us, a pair of kings.   Let's from this place.
What! look upon my brother: both your pardons,

146

That e'er I put between your holy looks
My ill suspicion.   This your son-in-law,
And son unto the king, whom heavens directing, 150
Is troth-plight to your daughter.   Good Paulina,
Lead us from hence, where we may leisurely
Each one demand, and answer to his part
Perform'd in this wide gap of time, since first
We were dissever'd: hastily lead away.   [*Exeunt.*

Glossary.

ABIDE, sojourn for a short time; "no more but a."=only make a short stay; IV. iii. 99.

ABOARD HIM, *i.e.* aboard his ship; IV. iv. 868.

ABUSED, deceived; II. i. 141.

ACTION, suit (perhaps "this a. I now go on"=this which I am now to undergo); II. i. 121.

ADDRESS YOURSELF, prepare; IV. iv. 53.

ADVENTURE, venture; I. ii. 38; II. iii. 162; dare, IV. iv. 470.

ADVENTURE of, risk of; V. i. 156.

AFAR OFF, indirectly; II. i. 104.

AFFECTION, instinct; I. ii. 138, disposition, V. ii. 40.

AFFRONT, confront, come before; V. i. 75.

AIR, breath; V. iii. 78.

"ALACK, FOR LESSER KNOWLEDGE"; *i.e.* "Oh, would that I had less knowledge"; II. i. 38.

ALLOW'D, allowable; I. ii. 263.

ALLOWING, approving; I. ii. 185.

AMAZEDLY, confusedly; V. i. 187.

AMAZEDNESS, amazement, surprise; V. ii. 5.

ANCIENT, old; IV. iv. 79.

ANCIENTRY, old people; III. iii. 63.

ANOTHER, the other; IV. iv. 176; V. ii. 82.

APE, imitator; V. ii. 108.

APE-BEARER, one who leads about apes; IV. iii. 101.

APPARENT, heir apparent; I. ii. 177.

APPOINT, dress; I. ii. 326.

APPOINTED, equipped; IV. iv. 603.

APPROBATION, attestation, confirmation; II. i. 177.

APPROVED, proved, tried; IV. ii. 32.

ASPECT, "the peculiar position and influence of a planet"; II. i. 107.

AT, (?) to; (perhaps "when at Bohemia you take my lord"="when you have my lord in Bohemia"); I. ii. 39.

AT FRIEND (so Folio 1; Folio 2, "as friend"), "on terms of friendship"; V. i. 140.

ATTACH, arrest; V. i. 182.

ATTORNEYED, performed by proxy; I. i. 30.

AUNTS, mistresses (*cp.* doxy); IV. iii. 11.

AVAILS, is of advantage; III. ii. 87.

AVOID, depart; I. ii. 462.

BAR, exclude; IV. iv. 440.

BARNE, a little child; III. iii. 71.

BASENESS, bastardy; II. iii. 78.

BASILISK, a fabulous serpent supposed to kill by its look; I. ii. 388.

BAWCOCK, a term of endearment (always masculine); I. ii. 121.

BEARING-CLOTH, "the mantle or cloth in which a child was carried to the font"; III. iii. 119.

BENCH'D, raised to authority; I. ii. 314.

BENTS, dispositions; I. ii. 179.

BIDE, dwell upon, repeat; I. ii. 242.

BLANK, "the white mark in the centre of a butt, the aim"; II. iii. 5.

BLENCH, start or fly off; I. ii. 333.

BLESS ME, preserve me; IV. iv. 271.

BLOCKS, blockheads; I. ii. 225.

BLUSTERS, boisterous tempests; III. iii. 4.

BOHEMIA=the king of B.; I. i. 7.

BOOT, avail; III. ii. 26.

BOOT, profit; IV. iv. 651; "grace to b.", "God help us"; I. ii. 80.

14 *l*

149

BORING, perforating; III. iii. 93.

BORROW, borrowing; I. ii. 39.

BOSOM, inmost thoughts; IV. iv. 574.

BOURN, limit, line of demarcation; I. ii. 12.

BRANDS, marks of infamy, stigmas; II. i. 71.

BRAVE, fine; IV. iv. 202.

BREAK-NECK, "dangerous business"; I. ii. 363.

BREED, educate; III. iii. 48.

BRING, take, accompany; IV. iii. 122.

BUG, bugbear; III. ii. 93.

BUGLE, a long bead of black glass; IV. iv. 224.

BUT, but that; V. i. 141.

BUT THAT, only because; II. i. 105.

BY-GONE DAY, day gone by=yesterday; I. ii. 32.

CADDISSES, worsted ribbons; IV. iv. 208.

CALLAT, a woman of bad character; II. iii. 90.

CAME HOME, "did not get hold"; (a nautical term) I. ii. 214.

CAP-A-PE, from head to foot; IV. iv. 761.

CAPARISON, literally horse-cloth; here used for "rags"; IV. iii. 27.

CARBONADOED, cut across for broiling; IV. iv. 268.

CARRIAGE, carrying on, management; III. i. 17.

CARVER, sculptor; V. iii. 30.

CENSURE, judgment; II. i. 37.

CENTRE, "the earth as the supposed centre of the world"; II. i. 90.

CHAMBER-COUNCILS, "private thoughts or intentions"; I. ii. 237.

CHANGED, exchanged; I. ii. 68.

CHANGELING, a child left by the fairies in the place of another; III. iii. 122.

CHARACTER, handwriting; V. ii. 38.

CHARGE, weight, value; IV. iv. 261.

CHEAT, (v. silly); IV. iii. 28.

CHILD, a girl; "a boy or a child" III. iii. 71.

CHILDNESS, childishness; I. ii. 170.

CHURL, peasant; IV. iv. 443.

CIRCUMSTANCE, ceremony, pomp; V. i. 90; facts which are evidence of the truth; V. ii. 33.

CLAMOUR (vide Note); IV. iv. 250.

CLAP, clap hands, i.e. pledge faith (a token of troth-plighting); I. ii. 104.

CLEAR'D, excepted; I. ii. 74.

CLERK-LIKE, scholar-like; I. ii. 392.

CLIMATE, reside, sojourn; V. i. 170.

CLIPPING, embracing; V. ii. 59.

COCK, woodcock, a metaphor for a fool; IV. iii. 36.

COLLOP, part of a man's flesh; I. ii. 137.

COLOUR, reason, pretext; IV. iv. 566.

COMFORTING, assisting; II. iii. 56.

COMFORTS, consolation; IV. iv. 563.

COMMEND, commit; II. iii. 182.

COMMISSION, warrant; I. ii. 144.

COMMODITY, advantage; III. ii. 94.

COMPASSED, gained possession of; IV. iii. 102.

CONCEIT, intelligence; I. ii. 224; idea; III. ii. 145.

CONCERNS, is of importance; III. ii. 87.

CONSIDERED, requited, paid; IV. iv. 825.

CONTENT, pleasure, delight; V. iii. 11.

CONTINENT, chaste; III. ii. 35.

CONTRACT, marriage-contract, espousals; V. i. 204.

CONTRARY, opposite side; I. ii. 372.

COPEST WITH, hast to do with; IV. iv. 435.

CORSE, corpse; IV. iv. 129.

COUNTERS, "a round piece of metal used in calculations"; IV. iii. 38.

COZENED, cheated; IV. iv. 254.

COZENERS, sharpers; IV. iv. 256.

CRACK, flaw; I. ii. 322.

CREDENT, credible; I. ii. 142.

CRONE, old woman; II. iii. 76.

CROWN IMPERIAL, the *Tritellaria imperialis*, early introduced from Constantinople into England; IV. iv. 126.

CURIOUS, requiring care, embarrassing; IV. iv. 525.

CURST, wicked; III. iii. 135.

CUSTOM, "with a c." from habit, IV. iv. 12; trade, custom, V. ii. 108.

CYPRESS, crape; IV. iv. 221.

DANCES, throbs; I. ii. 110.

DEAD, deadly; IV. iv. 445.

DEAR, devoted; II. iii. 150.

DELIVER, communicate; IV. iv. 509; narrate; V. ii. 4.

DELPHOS, Delphi; II. i. 183.

DENIED, refused; V. ii. 139.

DERIVATIVE, transmission by descent; III. ii. 45.

DIBBLE, "a pointed instrument to make holes for planting seeds"; IV. iv. 100.

DIE, gaming with the dice; IV. iii. 27.

DIFFERENCE, *i.e.* d. in our stations in life; IV. iv. 17.

DILDOS, a burden in popular songs; IV. iv. 195.

DIM, "violets dim," prob. "of quiet colour, not showy"; IV. iv. 120.

DISEASE, undress; IV. iv. 648.

DISCONTENTING, discontented; IV. iv. 543.

DISCOVER, disclose, shew; III. i. 20; communicate; IV. iv. 742.

DISCOVER'D, betrayed; II. i. 50.

DISCOVERY, disclosure; I. ii. 441.

DISLIKEN, disguise; IV. iv. 666.

DISPUTE, "discuss, reason upon"; IV. iv. 411.

DIS'S WAGGON, Pluto's chariot; IV. iv. 118.

DISTINGUISHMENT, distinction; II. i. 86.

DIVORCE, separation; IV. iv. 428.

DO, describe; V. ii. 63.

DOUBLE, doubly; V. iii. 107.

DOXY, mistress (a cant term); IV. iii. 2.

DRAB, a lewd woman; IV. iii. 27.

DREAD, apprehension; IV. iv. 17.

DREAD, awful, revered; I. ii. 322.

DREAMS, idle fancy; III. ii. 82.

DUNGY, filthy; II. i. 157.

EARNEST, earnest-money, handsel; IV. iv. 659.

"EGGS FOR MONEY," a proverbial expression; meaning to put up with an affront, or to act cowardly; I. ii. 161.

EMBRACEMENT, embrace; V. i. 114.

ENCOUNTER, behaviour; III. ii. 50.

ENCOUNTER, befall; II. i. 20.

ENFOLDINGS, garments; IV. iv. 756.

ESTATE, affairs; IV. iv. 411.

ESTATE, "unspeakable e.," *i.e.* great possessions; IV. ii. 46.

ETERNITY, immortality; V. ii. 106.

EXCREMENT, beard; IV. iv. 734.

EXTREMES, extravagance (of praise; and perhaps also in allusion to the extravagance of her attire); IV. iv. 6.

EYED, held in view; II. i. 35.

FADINGS, a common burden of songs; IV. iv. 195.

FAIL, failure; II. iii. 170; want, V. i. 27.

FALLING, letting fall; I. ii. 372.

FANCY, love; IV. iv. 493.

FARDEL (Folio "farthell"), pack, bundle; IV. iv. 728.

FASHION, kinds, sorts; III. ii. 105.

FAVOUR, countenance, look; V. ii. 53.

FEARFUL, full of fear; I. ii. 250.

FEATLY, neatly, adroitly; IV. iv. 176.

FEDERARY, accomplice; II. i. 90.

FEEDING, pasturage; IV. iv. 169.

FELLOWS, comrades; II. iii. 142.

FETCH OFF, "make away with"; I. ii. 334.

FIXURE, direction; V. iii. 67.

FLAP-DRAGONED, swallowed it like a flap-dragon (*i.e.* snap-dragon); III. iii. 100.

FLATNESS, completeness; III. ii. 123.

FLAUNTS, finery, showy apparel; IV. iv. 23.

FLAX-WENCH, a woman whose occupation is to dress flax; I. ii. 277.

FLAYED, stripped, skinned; IV. iv. 655.

FLOWER-DE-LUCE, fleur-de-lys (it is uncertain whether Shakespeare was thinking of a lily or an iris); IV. iv. 127.

FOND, foolish; IV. iv. 437.

FOOLS, "a term of endearment and pity"; II. i. 118.

FOR, because; III. i. 4; IV. iv. 86.

FOR BECAUSE, because; II. i. 7.

FORCE, necessity; IV. iv. 434.

FORCED, strained, far-fetched (or "mistaken"); IV. iv. 41.

FORCEFUL, strong; II. i. 163.

'FORE, before; III. ii. 42.

FOREFEND, forbid; IV. iv. 541.

FORGES, causes, produces; IV. iv. 17.

FORK'D, horned; I. ii. 186.

FRAMED, planned, pre-arranged; V. i. 91.

FRANKLINS, yeomen; V. ii. 173.

FRAUGHT, freighted, burdened; IV. iv. 525.

FREE, noble (perhaps voluntary); II. ii. 44; guiltless, II. iii. 30; accessible to all, II. i. 194; eager, ready, IV. iv. 559.

FRESH, youthful; IV. iv. 433; IV. iv. 562.

FRIENDS, "these unknown f. to's"; these friends unknown to us; IV. iv. 65.

FRIENDSHIPS, kind services; IV. ii. 22.

FROM, away from; IV. ii. 43.

FURNISH'D, equipped, fitted out; IV. iv. 599.

GALL'D, harassed, injured; I. ii. 316.

GALLIMAUFRY, medley, hotch-potch; IV. iv. 335.

GALLOWS, *i.e.* the fear or risk of the g.; IV. iii. 28.

GENTLE, adjective used substantively = gentle one, IV. iv. 46; gentlemen, I. ii. 394.

GENTLY, kindly; IV. iv. 825.

GENTRY, birth; I. ii. 393.

GERMANE, akin, related; IV. iv. 802.

GEST, appointed stages of a royal progress, hence the fixed limit of a visit; I. ii. 41.

GILLYVORS, gillyflowers; a variety of the carnation; IV. iv. 82.

GIVE OUT, proclaim; IV. iv. 149.

GLASS, hour-glass; I. ii. 306.

GLISTERS, shines, sparkles; III. ii. 171.

GLOVES; "g. as sweet as damask roses"; alluding to the custom of perfuming gloves; IV. iv. 222.

GO ABOUT, intend; IV. iv. 219; attempt, IV. iv. 720.

GOAL, point at issue; I. ii. 96.

GOOD DEED, in very deed; I. ii. 42.

GORGE, stomach; II. i. 44.

GOSSIPS, sponsors; II. iii. 41.

GRACE, favour; III. ii. 48.

GRACIOUS, prosperous, III. i. 22; endowed with grace, III. ii. 30.

GRAFTED IN MY SERIOUS TRUST, trusted without reserve, absolutely; I. ii. 246.

GUST, taste, perceive; I. ii. 219.

GUILTY TO, chargeable for; IV. iv. 549.

HALED, dragged; III. ii. 102.

HAMMER'D OF, pondered upon; II. ii. 49.

HAND, lay hands on; II. iii. 63.

HAND-FAST, custody, confinement; IV. iv. 795.

HANGMAN, executioner; IV. iv. 468.

"HAPPY MAN BE'S DOLE," a proverbial expression = "May his dole or share in life be to be a happy man"; I. ii. 163.

HARLOT, lewd; II. iii. 4.

HAVE, possess; IV. iv. 574.

HAVE AT, I'll try; IV. iv. 302.

HAVING, possessions, property; IV. iv. 741.

HEAT, traverse (as at a race); I. ii. 96.

HEAVINGS, sighs; II. iii. 35.

HEAVY, sad, sorrowful; III. iii. 115.

HEFTS, retchings; II. i. 45.

HENT, pass beyond; IV. iii. 133.

HEREDITARY, _i.e._ derived from our first parents (alluding to "original sin"); I. ii. 75.

HIM, by him, (? the man); I. ii. 412.

HOLY, pious, good, V. i. 170; blameless, V. iii. 148.

HOME, out, to the end; I. ii. 248; fully, V. iii. 4.

HONEST, chaste, virtuous; II. i. 68.

HOT, active; IV. iv. 699.

HOVERING, "irresloute, wavering"; I. ii. 302.

HOXES, hamstrings; I. ii. 244.

I' FECKS, in fact; I. ii. 120.

IMMODEST, immoderate; III. ii. 103.

IMPAWN'D, in pledge; I. ii. 436.

IMPORTANCE, import; V. ii. 20.

INCENSE, incite; V. i. 61.

INCERTAIN, uncertain; V. i. 29.

INCERTAINTIES, "accidents of fortune"; III. ii. 170.

INCIDENCY, "a falling on"; I. ii. 403.

INCONSTANT, fickle; III. ii. 187.

INDUSTRIOUSLY, "deliberately"; I. ii. 256.

INJURY OF TONGUES, mischief caused by scandal; I. ii. 338.

INKLE, a kind of tape; IV. iv. 208.

INSINUATE, intermeddle; IV. iv. 760.

INSTIGATION, incitement; II. i. 163.

INTELLIGENCING, carrying intelligence; II. iii. 68.

INTELLIGENT, communicative; I. ii. 378.

INTENTION, aim; I. ii. 138.

IRREMOVEABLE, immovable; IV. iv. 518.

IT IS, he is; I. i. 38.

JAR, tick; I. ii. 43.

JEWEL, personal ornament of gold or precious stones; V. ii. 36.

JULIO ROMANO (v. Note); V. ii. 105.

JUSTIFIED, confirmed, ratified; V. iii. 145.

JUSTIFY HIM, confirm his assertion; V. ii. 71.

KILN-HOLE, the opening of an oven; probably the fire-place used in making malt; a noted gossiping place; IV. iv. 247.

KNACKS, knick-knacks; IV. iv. 360.

KNOCK, cuffs, blows; IV. iii. 29.

LAND, nation; IV. iv. 8.

LAND-DAMN (_vide_ Note); II. i. 143.

LASTING, everlasting, eternal; I. ii. 317.

LAY ME, bury me; IV. iv. 468.

LAYS ON, does it in good style; IV. iii. 43.

LEAN TO, incline, tend towards; II. i. 64.

LET, let remain; I. ii. 41.

LEVEL, direction of, aim; III. ii. 82.

'LEVEN, eleven; IV. iii. 33.

LIST, care, choose; IV. i. 26.

LIST, listen, hearken; IV. iv. 552.

LIKE, likely; II. ii. 27.

LIKE, "an' it like," if it please; IV. iv. 737.

LIMBER, flexible, easy bent I. ii. 47.

LIMIT, "strength of l." limited strength; III. ii. 107.

LIVELY, naturally; V. iii. 19.

LOOK OUT; "makes her blood l.o.," *i.e.* makes her blush; IV. iv. 160.

LOOK UPON, take notice of; IV. ii. 41.

LORDINGS, lordlings; I. ii. 62.

LOSS, be discarded; II. iii. 192.

LOUD, tempestuous; III. iii. 11.

LOWER MESSES, "persons of inferior rank" (properly those who sat at the lower end of the table); I. ii. 227.

LOZEL, cowardly fellow; II. iii. 109.

LUNES, mad freaks; II. ii. 30.

LUSTY, lively, active; II. ii. 27.

MAIDENHEADS, maidenhoods; IV. iv. 116.

MANKIND, masculine; II. iii. 67.

MANNERLY, decent; II. i. 86.

MARBLE; "most m." the most hard-hearted; V. iii. 98.

MARGERY, a term of contempt; II. iii. 160.

MARK, pattern; IV. iv. 8.

MARTED, traded; IV. iv. 363.

MARVEL, astonishment; V. i. 188.

MASTERS, well-wishers, patrons; V. ii. 188.

MEANER FORM, lower position; I. ii. 313.

MEANS, tenors or counter-tenors; IV. iii. 46.

MEASURE, stately tread; IV. iv. 756.

MEASURE, judge of; II. i. 114.

MEDICINE, physician; IV. iv. 598.

MEDLER, busybody; IV. iv. 329.

MEET, proper, fit; II. ii. 46.

MEN OF HAIR, dressed in goat-skins to resemble satyrs; IV. iv. 333.

MERE, absolute; III. ii. 142; only, III. ii. 145.

MESS, course (of a feast); IV. iv. 11.

MIDWIFE, old woman, used contemptuously; II. iii. 160.

MOE, more; I. ii. 8.

MOIETY, part, portion; II. iii. 8; half, III. ii. 40.

MORTAL, fatal; III. ii. 149.

MORT O' THE DEER, a note blown at the death of the deer; I. ii. 118.

MOTION, puppet show; IV. iii. 103.

NAYWARD, contradiction; II. i. 64.

NEAR, like, resembling; V. ii. 109.

NEAT, used with a quibble upon "neat"=horned cattle; I. ii. 123.

NEAT-HERDS, cow-keepers; IV. iv. 332.

NEB, beak=mouth; I. ii. 183.

NECKLACE AMBER, "an amber of which necklaces were made, commonly called 'bead-amber,' fit to perfume a lady's chamber"; IV. iv. 224.

NEXT, nearest; III. iii. 128.

NOTE, mark, sign, I. ii. 287; knowledge, I. i. 40; distinction, eminence, IV. ii. 48; mark for measuring time; "shepherd's note"=the shepherd hath observed, noted, I. ii. 2.

NOTED, respected; V. iii. 145.

O'ERWEEN, am overbold, presume; IV. ii. 9.

OF, off (=on); "browzing of ivy"; III. iii. 69.

OF, some of; "you have of," *i.e.* there are some; IV. iv. 217.

OFFICED, "having a place or function"; I. ii. 172.

O' LIFE (Folio "a life"), on my life; IV. iv. 264.

ON, of; II. ii. 23.

ON'T, of it; II. i. 169.

OUT, on the wrong scent; II. i. 72.

OUT OF, without; V. i. 90.

OVER, over us; IV. iv. 668.

OVERTURE, disclosure; II. i. 172.

PADDLING PALMS, toying with hands; used contemptuously; I. ii. 115.

PALE, paleness (with probably a play on the other sense, limit, boundary); IV. iii. 4.

PANDAR, go-between; II. i. 46.

PANTLER, the servant who had charge of the pantry; IV. iv. 56.

PARAGON, pattern of supreme excellence; V. i. 153.

PART, depart; I. ii. 10; divide; I. ii. 18.

PARTAKE, communicate; V. iii. 132.

PARTLET; "Dame P." alluding to Chaucer's *Nonne Prestes Tale*, where P. is the name of the favourite hen of Chauntecleer; II. iii. 75.

PARTS, actions, tasks; I. ii. 400.

PASH, head; I. ii. 128.

PASSES, surpasses; II. ii. 20.

PASSING, surpassing; IV. iv. 294.

PATTERN, match; III. ii. 37.

PAY YOUR FEES; alluding to fees paid by prisoners, whether guilty or not, on their liberation; I. ii. 53.

PEER, peep out; IV. iii. 1.

PEERING, disclosing (herself); IV. iv. 3.

PERFECT, sure; III. iii. 1.

PERFORMED, executed; V. ii. 105.

PETTITOES, pigs' feet; used contemptuously; IV. iv. 619.

PHYSICS, heals, cures; I. i. 43.

PICTURE, appearance; IV. iv. 615; painted statue; V. ii. 187.

PIECE, complete; V. ii. 117.

PIECE UP, hoard up, so as to have his fill; V. iii. 56.

PIEDNESS, variegation; IV. iv. 87.

PIN AND WEB, the disease of the eyes, now known as cataract; I. ii. 291.

PINCH'D, made ridiculous; II. i. 51.

PLACES, position, station; I. ii. 448.

PLACKETS, some special article of female attire; IV. iv. 245.

PLUCKING, pulling; IV. iv. 476.

POINTS, tagged laces for fastening

various articles of attire; here an obvious play on the word; IV. iv. 206.

POKING-STICKS, small iron, brass, or silver rods, which were heated, and used for setting the plaits of ruffs; IV. iv. 228.

POMANDER, "a ball composed of perfumes"; IV. iv. 609.

PONDEROUS, forcible; IV. iv. 535.

POST; "in p." in haste; II. i. 182.

POSTERNS, the smaller gates of a city; I. ii. 438.

POUND AND ODD SHILLING, twenty-one shillings, a guinea; IV iii. 34.

POWER; "to my p." to the best of my power; V. ii. 182.

POWERFUL, forcible, hence "deterrent"; IV. iii. 29.

PRACTICE, artifice, device; III. ii. 168.

PRANK'D UP, decked up, adorned; IV. iv. 10.

PREDOMINANT, used as an astrological term; I. ii. 202.

PREGNANT, made plausible; V. ii. 33.

PREPOSTEROUS, Clown's blunder for *prosperous;* V. ii. 158.

PRESENT, immediate; II. iii. 184.

PRESENTLY, immediately; II. i. 47.

PRETENCE, purpose, intention; III. ii. 18.

PRIG, thief; IV. iii. 108.

PROFESS, confess, own; IV. iv. 550.

PROFESS'D, professed friendship; I. ii. 456.

PROPER, own; II. iii. 139.

PUGGING, thievish; IV. iii 7.

PURCHASED, gained, came to; IV. iii. 27.

PURGATION, exculpation; III. ii. 7.

PURITAN, a contemptuous allusion to the "Psalm-singing Puritans"; IV. iii. 46.

PUSH, impulse, impetus; V. iii. 129.

PUTTER-ON, instigator ; II. i. 141.

QUALIFY, appease, soften ; IV. iv. 543.
QUESTION, conversation ; IV. ii. 55 ;
"in q.," under examination, trial,
V. i. 198.
QUICK, alive ; IV. iv. 132.
QUOIFS, caps, hoods ; IV. iv. 226.

RACE, root ; IV. iii. 50.
RASH, quick, sudden ; I. ii. 319.
REAR'D, raised ; I. ii. 314.
REASON, it is just ; IV. iv. 417.
REGARD, look ; I. ii. 390.
RELISH, realize, perceive ; II. i. 167.
REMEMBER, remind ; III. ii. 231.
REMOVED, retired, sequestered ; V. ii.
116.
REMOVEDNESS, retirement : II. ii. 41.
REPAIR, restoration ; V. i. 31.
REPLENISH'D, perfect ; II. i. 79.
REQUIRE, deserve, II. iii. 190 ; III. ii.
64.
RESOLVE YOU, prepare yourselves,
compose yourselves ; V. iii. 86.
RESPECTING, considering ; V. i. 35.
REVEREND, "venerable, entitled to
high respect" ; IV. iv. 73.
REVIEW, re-view, see again : IV. iv.
680.
RHEUMS, rheumatism ; IV. iv. 410.
RIFT, burst, split ; V. i. 66.
RIPE, pressing ; I. ii. 332.
ROSEMARY, referred to as the symbol
of remembrance ; IV. iv. 74.
ROUNDING, murmuring ; I. ii. 217.
RUE. referred to as the herb of grace ;
IV. iv. 74.

SAD, serious, earnest ; IV. iv. 316.
SAFFRON, a spice used for colouring
paste ; IV. iii. 48.
SALTIERS, the servant's blunder for
satyrs ; IV. iv. 334.
SAP, life, hope ; IV. iv. 576.
SAVOUR, smell, scent ; IV. iv. 75.

SCAPE, transgression ; III. iii. 73.
SEALING, closing, putting an end to ;
I. ii. 337.
SEAR, brand ; II. i. 73.
SECOND ; "be second to me," second
my efforts ; II. iii. 27.
SEEMING, appearance ; IV. iv. 75.
SEEMS, appears ; IV. iv. 157.
SEIZED, fallen on, overpowered ; V. i.
142.
SEVEN-NIGHT, week ; I. ii. 17.
SEVERALS, individuals ; I. ii. 226.
SHALL 'S, shall us (i.e. shall we ; "shall"
perhaps used impersonally) ; I. ii.
178.
SHE, love, mistress ; IV. iv. 360.
SHEEP - WHISTLING, whistling after
sheep, tending sheep ; IV. iv. 805.
SHEETS ; "is sheets," i.e. is to steal s. ;
IV. iii. 23.
SHORE, put ashore ; IV. iv. 869.
SHOULD, would ; I. ii. 57.
'SHREW, beshrew, a mild form of im-
precation ; I. ii. 281.
SIGHTED, having eyes ; I. ii. 388.
SILLY ; "s. cheat," harmless fraud,
petty thievery ; IV. iii. 28.
SINCE, when ; V. i. 219.
SINGULAR, unique ; IV. iv. 144.
SINGULARITIES, rarities, curiosities ;
V. iii. 12.
SITTING, interview ; IV. iv. 572.
SKILL, cunning ; II. i. 166 ; reason,
motive (or rather a thought caused
by consideration and judgment) ;
IV. iv. 152.
SLEEVE-HAND, wristband. cuff ; IV.
iv. 212.
SNEAPING, nipping ; I. ii. 13.
SOFTLY, slowly ; IV. iii. 121.
SOAKING, absorbent ; I. ii. 224.
SOLELY, alone ; II. iii. 17.
SOOTH ; "good s." in very truth ; IV.
iv. 160.
SO THAT, provided that : II. i. 9.
SPED, prospered, succeeded ; I. ii. 389.

156

SPEED, fortune; III. ii. 146.

SPICES, seasonings; III. ii. 185.

SPLITT'ST, cleav'st; I. ii. 349.

SPOKE, spoken; I. ii. 106.

SPRIGHTLY, in a sprightly manner (adjective in *-ly* used as adverb); IV. iv. 53.

SPRINGE, a noose for catching birds; IV. iii. 36.

SQUARE, the embroidery on the bosom of a garment; IV. iv. 212.

SQUARED, shaped; V. i. 52.

SQUASH, an unripe peascod; I. ii. 160.

SQUIER, square measure; IV. iv. 348.

STAND, fight; III. ii. 46.

STAR; "the watery star," the moon; I. ii. 1.

STARR'D, fated; III. ii. 100.

STATE, estate, rank, station; IV. iv. 437.

STRAIGHT, straightway, immediately; II. i. 70.

STRAIN'D, turned from the right course; III. ii. 51.

STRAITED, at a loss; IV. iv. 365.

STRANGELY, as if it were a stranger; II. iii. 182.

STRETCH - MOUTHED, broad - spoken; IV. iv. 196.

STRONG, forcible; I. ii. 34.

STUFF'D, complete; II. i. 185.

SUBJECT, people; I. ii. 43.

SUCCESS, succession; I. ii. 394.

SUDDENLY, immediately; II. iii. 200.

SUFFICIENCY, ability; II. i. 185.

SWEAR OVER, endeavour to overcome by swearing oaths; I. ii. 424.

TABLE-BOOK, tablet, memorandum book; IV. iv. 610.

TAKE, excite, move; III. ii. 38.

TAKE IN, conquer, take; IV. iv. 588.

TALL; "t. fellow of thy hands," active, able-bodied man who will bear the test; V. ii. 177.

TARDIED, retarded; III. ii. 163.

TAWDRY-LACE, a rustic necklace (said to be corrupted from St Audrey, *i.e.* St Ethelreda, on whose day, the 17th October, a fair was held in the isle of Ely, where gay toys of all sorts were sold); IV. iv. 253.

TELL, count; IV. iv. 185.

TENDER, show, introduce; IV. iv. 826.

THAT=O that! (or better, dependent on "I am question'd by my fears"; "that . . . no"="lest"); I. ii. 12.

THAT, so that; I. i. 32; provided that, I. ii. 84, 85.

THEREABOUTS, of that import; I. ii. 378.

THERETO, added thereto, besides; I. ii. 391.

THICK, make thick, thicken; I. ii. 171.

THOUGHT, idea, opinion; I. ii. 424.

THOUGHT ON, held in estimation; IV. iv. 531.

"THREE MAN SONG-MEN," *i.e.* "singers of songs in three parts"; IV. iii. 45.

THREE-PILE, the richest and most costly kind of velvet; IV. iii. 14.

THRIVING, successful; II. ii. 45.

TINCTURE, colour; III. ii. 206.

TOAZE (Folio 1, "at toaze"), "probably to touse, *i.e.* pull, tear"; IV. iv. 760.

TOD, twenty-eight pounds of wool; IV. iii. 34.

TODS, yields a tod; IV. iii. 33.

TRAFFIC, business, trade; IV. iii. 23.

TRAITORLY, traitrous; IV. iv. 821.

TRANSPORTED, hurried away by violent passion; III. ii. 159; borne away by ecstacy; V. iii. 69.

TREMOR CORDIS, trembling of the heart; I. ii. 110.

TRICK, toy, plaything; II. i. 51.

TROLL-MY-DAMES, the French game of *Trou-madame*; IV. iii. 92.

TRUMPET, trumpeter, herald; II. ii. 35.

TRUNK, body ; I. ii. 435.

TUG, strive, struggle ; IV. iv. 508.

TURTLES, turtle-doves ; IV. iv. 154.

UNBRAIDED, (?)= "not counterfeit, sterling, but probably the Clown's blunder for *embroidered*" ; IV. iv. 204.

UNCLASP'D, revealed ; III. ii. 168.

UNCURRENT, objectionable, unallowable (like false coin) ; III. ii. 50.

UNDERGO, undertake ; IV. iv. 554.

UNEASY, difficult ; IV. ii. 56.

UNFURNISH, deprive ; V. i. 123.

UNINTELLIGENT, ignorant, unconscious ; I. i 16.

UNROLLED, struck off the rolls (of thieves) ; IV. iii. 130.

UNSPHERE, remove from their orbs ; I ii. 48.

UNTHRIFTY, not increasing ; V. ii. 120.

UNVENERABLE, contemptible ; II. iii. 77.

URGENT, pressing ; I. ii. 465.

USE : " the u. on 't," having been used ; III. i. 14.

UTTER, " cause to pass from one to another " ; IV. iv. 330.

VAST (later Folios "a vast sea)", a boundless sea ; I. i. 33.

VESSEL, creature ; III. iii. 21.

VICE, screw, force ; I. ii. 416.

VILLAIN, a term of endearment ; I. ii. 136.

VIRGINALLING, "playing as upon a virginal (a sort of small pianoforte)"; I. ii. 125.

VISIBLE, appearing visibly ; V. i. 216.

VISITATION, visit ; I. i. 7 ; IV. iv. 566.

VULGARS, the common people ; II. i. 94.

WAFTING, turning quickly ; I. ii. 372.

WAITS UPON, accompanies ; V. i. 142.

WANT, be without ; IV. ii. 15.

WANTON, play ; II. i. 18.

WARD, " guard made in fencing " ; I. ii. 33.

WARDEN, a baking pear ; IV. iii. 48.

WEARING, apparel, dress ; IV. iv. 9.

WEEDS, garments ; IV. iv. 1.

WELKIN, heavenly, (?) blue ; I. ii. 136.

WELL, at rest ; V. i. 30.

WHAT, whatever ; I. ii. 44.

WHICH, that which ; III. ii. 61.

WHISTLE OFF (Folio 1, whistle of) ; perhaps, derived from falconry ; " to whistle off "= to send off ; IV. iv. 247.

WHOO-BUB, outcry, clamour ; IV. iv. 629.

" WHOOP, DO ME NO HARM, GOODMAN," the name of an old song ; IV. iv. 199.

WILD, rash ; II. i. 182.

WILFUL-NEGLIGENT, wilfully negligent ; I. ii. 255.

WINK, the act of closing the eyes ; I. ii. 317.

WINKED, closed my eyes ; III. iii. 106.

WINNERS, " precious w." winners of things precious to you ; V. iii. 131.

WIT, wisdom ; II. ii. 52.

WITH, by ; IV. iii. 27 ; V. ii. 68.

WITHOUT-DOOR, outward, external ; II. i. 69.

WOMAN-TIRED, hen-pecked ; II. iii. 74.

WONDER, admiration ; V. i. 133.

WONDERING, admiration ; IV. i. 25.

WORN, spent ; " w. times," spent youth= old age ; V. i. 142.

WORSHIP, honour, dignity ; I. ii. 314.

WORTH, worthiness of all kinds, here especially fortune and rank ; V. i. 214.

WOTTING, knowing ; III. ii. 77.

WROUGHT, worked upon, agitated ; V. iii. 58.

YELLOW, the colour of jealousy ; II. iii. 106.

YEST, spume or foam of water ; III. iii. 94.

YET, still ; I. ii. 51.

Notes.

I. ii. 44. '*What lady she her lord*'; 'she' has been variously interpreted; Collier and Dyce proposed 'should,' destroying the beauty of the line; Schmidt makes the phrase 'lady she'='a woman that is a lady,' taking 'she'='woman'; others print 'lady-she'; perhaps the word may be best explained as the pleonastic pronoun so common in popular poetry; the rhythm seems to favour this latter view.

I. ii. 70. '*The doctrine of ill-doing, nor dream'd*'; so Folio 1; the later Folios, '*no, nor dream'd*'; Spedding, '*neither dream'd*'; perhaps '*doctrine*' should be read as a trisyllable; a harsh line would, however, result; and the reading of the later Folios has much to commend it.

I. ii. 131-2. '*false As o'er-dyed blacks*'; Folios 1, 2, 3, '*o're dy'd*'; the words have been variously interpreted to mean 'fabrics dyed over with some other colour,' or, 'dyed too much'; Steevens saw in the phrase an allusion to the fact that black will receive no other hue without discovering itself through it; the passage may simply contain the idea, 'the blacker the garb, the less sincere the mourning.'

I. ii. 154. '*methoughts*'; so the Folios in this and other places; this erroneous form was probably due to '*methinks*'; it is noteworthy that the correct '*methought*' occurs a few lines below.

I. ii. 284. '*that*,' *i.e.* 'that of which you accuse her.'

II. i. 11. '*Who taught you this?*' Rowe's emendation of the

159

reading of Folio 1, '*taught 'this*' (with an apostrophe before '*this*,' indicating an elision); the later Folios, '*taught this.*'

II. i. 25. '*A sad tale's best for winter* ', hence the title of the play.

II. i. 39-41. '*There may be in the cup A spider*,' etc.; it was formerly believed that spiders were venomous.

II. i. 134. '*I'll keep my stables where I lodge my wife* '; i.e. 'I'll degrade my wife's chamber into a stable or dog kennel.'

II. i. 143. '*I would land-damn him*'; so the Folios; '*land-damm*,' '*laudanum*,' '*lamback*,' (i.e. 'beat'), '*half-damn*,' '*live-damn*,' '*landan (lantan, rantan)*,' '*lant-dam*,' are among the various emendations proposed; Schmidt suggests '*I would—Lord, damn him !*' In all probability the reading of the Folios should not be departed from, and it seems likely that Antigonus, having in the previous phrase used the word '*damn'd*,' here uses '*land-damn*,' as a sort of grim quibble for '*landan*,'—a Gloucestershire word still in use " to express the punishment meted out to slanderers and adulterers by rustics traversing from house to house along the country side, blowing trumpets and beating drums or pans and kettles ; when an audience was assembled the delinquents' names were proclaimed, and they were said to be landanned " (*cp.* Halliwell's *Dictionary of Archaic Words*, and *Notes and Queries* iii. 464): *landan, lantan, rantan*, were variants of the same word, which was probably imitative in its origin.

II. i. 153. '*As you feel doing thus*,' probably = my doing thus to you (*i.e.* touching him, or perhaps pulling his beard); '*the instruments that feel*' = my fingers.

II. iii. 178. '*to it own protection* ' so Folios 1, 2 ; Folios 3, 4, '*its* '; the old possessive form '*it*,' still in use in Lancashire, occurs again in this play (III. ii. 101); there are some dozen instances elsewhere : '*it own*,' may be regarded as a sort of idiomatic compound, the combination helping to maintain the archaism ; '*its* (Folio, *it's*) *own*,' to be found in Act I ii. 266 is said to be the only instance of its use in Shakespeare.

III. iii. 124. '*You're a made old man*'; Theodald's emendation of the Folio reading '*mad*,' confirmed by a passage in Shakespeare's original :—"The goodman desired her to be quiet . . if she could hold her peace they were made for ever."

IV. i. 15. '*to it*,' *i.e.* 'the present.'

IV. ii. 4. '*It is fifteen years since*,' etc.; changed by Hanmer to '*sixteen*,' the number intended by Shakespeare.

IV. iii. 23. '*when the kite builds, look to lesser linen*'; alluding to this bird's habit of carrying off small linen garments hung out to dry; Autolycus preferred more substantial prey.

IV. iii. 54. '*I' the name of me* ——'; probably, as has been suggested, the Clown's exclamation of '*Mercy*' is interrupted by Autolycus.

IV. iv. 250. '*clamour your tongues*'; Hanmer's emendation '*charm*' has been generally adopted, but '*clamour*' is almost certainly correct (Taylor, the Water-Poet, wrote '*Clamour the promulgation of your tongues*') ; '*clamour*' or rather '*clammer*,' is probably radically identical with '*clamber*,' the Scandinavian original of which '*klambra*'= 'to pinch closely together, to clamp.'

IV iv. 279. '*another ballad of a fish*'; *cp. e.g.* "A strange report of a monstrous fish that appeared in the form of a woman from her waist upward, seen in the sea"; entered in the Stationers' Registers in 1604.

IV. iv. 442. '*Far than Deucalion off*'; '*far*'= 'farther'; the Folios all correctly read '*farre*,' *i.e.* the old form of the comparative of '*far*.'

IV. iv. 592. '*i' the rear o' her birth*'; Folios 1, 2, 3, '*our birth*'; Rowe first emended the line as in the text, though in his second edition he read '*o' our*' for '*o' her.*'

IV. iv. 600. '*appear,*' *i.e.* appear so (like Bohemia's son).

IV. iv. 731. '*at palace*'; Folio 1, '*at 'Pallace*''; probably the apostrophe indicates "the omission of the article or its absorption in rapid pronunciation."

V. ii. 60. '*weather-bitten conduit*'; changed to '*weather-beaten*' in Folio 3; but '*weather-bitten*' is undoubtedly the correct form (*cp.* Skeat's *Etymological Dictionary*): *conduits* were frequently in the form of human figures.

V. ii. 105. '*that rare Italian master*'; Giulio Pippi, known as 'Giulio Romano,' was born in 1492, and died in 1546; his fame as a painter was widespread; Shakespeare, taking him as '*a type of artistic excellence,*' makes him a sculptor; it must, however, be remembered that the statue was a '*painted picture.*' Much has been made of this reference by the advocates of Shakespeare's alleged Italian journeys (*cp.* Elze's *Essays on Shakespeare*).

*Printed in Great Britain
by Turnbull & Spears, Edinburgh*